D0794611

LIBRARY MEDIA CENTER
ALBUQUERQUE ACADEMY

NEW MEXICO

PORTRAIT OF THE LAND AND THE PEOPLE

BY JULIE KIRGO

AMERICAN GEOGRAPHIC PUBLISHING

WILLIAM A. CORDINGLEY, CHAIRMAN
RICK GRAETZ, PUBLISHER & CEO
MARK O. THOMPSON, DIRECTOR OF PUBLICATIONS
BARBARA FIFER, PRODUCTION MANAGER

DENNIS & MARIA HENRY   INSET: STEPHEN TRIMBLE

ISBN 0-938314-65-3

© 1989 American Geographic
Publishing
P.O. Box 5630
Helena, MT 59604
(406) 443-2842

text © 1989 Julie Kirgo
Design by Linda Collins
Printed in Hong Kong

Julie Kirgo has worked as a tele-vision writer for the past 12 years, and has been an editor at *TV Guide* and the Los Angeles edi-tion of *Where* magazine. As a freelance journalist, she has con-tributed to publications ranging from the Los Angeles *Times* to *The Saturday Evening Post*.

American Geographic Publishing is a corporation for publishing illus-trated geographic information and guides. It is not associated with American Geographical Society. It has no commercial or legal relation-ship to and should not be confused with any other company, society or group using the words geographic or geographical in its name or its publications.

TOM TILL

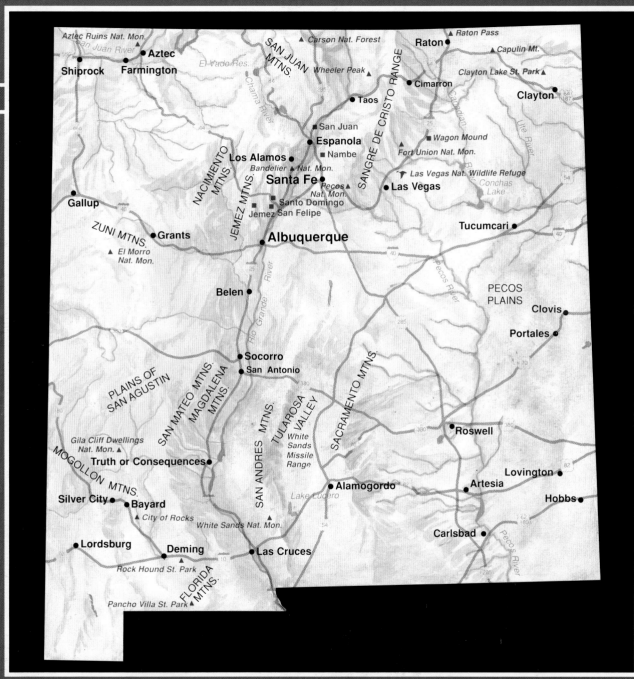

LINDA COLLINS

CONTENTS

Facing page, top: The old-world look of
Cerillos, central New Mexico.
Bottom: *Feast Day participant, San Juan
Pueblo.*
Right: *La Ventana, the largest natural arch
in New Mexico.*

Title page: *A yucca stands sentinel over
sunrise-swept dunes, White Sands National
Monument.* DENNIS & MARIA HENRY

Front cover: *Enchanted Mesa, Acoma Pueblo.*
STEPHEN TRIMBLE

Back cover, left: *Shiprock.* DAN PEHA
Right top: *Christmas Eve, San Felipe de Neri,
Albuquerque.* JONATHAN A. MEYERS
Right bottom: *Comanche at San Juan Pueblo
feast day.* STEPHEN TRIMBLE

DENNIS & MARIA HENRY

INTRODUCTION

To my everlasting regret, I am not a native of New Mexico. But, like so many others, I have found my heart's home in "The Land of Enchantment"—a boosterish name for a place which, I have come to believe, merits it quite literally.

I first visited the state briefly as a child of 12, whisked with my sister and brother from the stuffy confines of the Santa Fe Chief through narrow streets drenched with a strange bright light into the shadowy oasis of a thick-walled adobe restaurant. Our rowdiness somehow stilled by the venerable atmosphere, the cool hush of that room, we ate—with unlikely docility—a meal of shockingly spicy food. And that was all; one hour in Albuquerque, and it was on to Los Angeles.

But the memory of that dim old room, of the clear thin light pressing against the window panes, stayed with me; so much so that I jumped at a chance to visit New Mexico again some 10 years later. This time I traveled by car, coming in from the West past the long ranks of high red cliffs outside Gallup, then on again into Albuquerque, where, once more, I found myself quieting under the spell of the cool room, the fiery food and the high, clear light. By the time I had pushed north to wander the low brown town of Santa Fe, to see the stirring blue silhouette of Taos Mountain rearing over its high plateau, I was bewitched: what had seemed, in memory, like a mirage, was presented to me as a reality more solid, more intense than anything I could have imagined.

New Mexico has never let me down; the strange, wild beauty of its shimmering plains, deeply gashed canyons and long blue mountain reaches has not dimmed through the years of our acquaintance. Not everyone, it must be noted, will share my passion; the state's emptiness can be frightening, its exotic atmosphere intimidating. Many visitors lose their bearings as they cross the border, becoming convinced that they can no longer be on American soil; *New Mexico Magazine* runs a monthly feature entitled "One of Our Fifty Is Missing," recounting tales of tourists who offer to pay for meals in pesos, of telephone operators who insist that calls to New Mexico be prefaced by an overseas dialing code. And in

1864, General William Tecumseh Sherman spoke for generations of the disgruntled when he advised the government about the recently acquired Territory of New Mexico: he urged that a diplomatic effort be launched to "prevail upon Mexico to take it back."

But the malcontents are in the minority. Over the centuries, the state has claimed the hearts (and enthralled the imaginations) of Indians and conquistadors, mountain men and miners, cowboys and homesteaders—the whole vast colorful panoply of the West, up to and including the tourists of our own day, many of whom have come to visit, lingered, and finally settled in for a lifetime. Particularly over the last century, New Mexico has been a magnet for artists, writers and others of a creative bent, most of whom have tried, at one point or another, to capture the source of the region's charm. D.H. Lawrence perhaps struck closest to the heart when he rhapsodized, "For a greatness of beauty I have never experienced anything like New Mexico...the moment I saw the brilliant, proud morning shine high up over the deserts of Santa Fe, something stood still in my soul, and I started to attend. There was a certain magnificence in the high-up day, a certain eagle-like royalty...In the magnificent fierce morning of New Mexico one sprang awake, a new part of the soul woke up suddenly, and the old world gave way to a new."

Oliver La Farge, on the other hand, may have been more honest, writing that New Mexico is "a land that draws and holds men and women with ties that cannot be explained or submitted to reason." For the region's charms, while easy to feel, are hard to describe. Sheer physical beauty is there, of course, in abundance: in the unfettered space, in colors both delicate and harsh, in that clarity of light which mounts, finally, to the mystical. The state's history is long (Spaniards founded Santa Fe before the Pilgrims dreamed of Plymouth Rock, and they did so in the midst of Indians who had been farming the fertile terraces of the Rio Grande for centuries), difficult and colorful in the best traditions of the dime novel and the movie Western; it is also ever-present, alive in the shadowy hush of a mission church, on the sun-baked plaza of an Indian pueblo, amidst the eerie ruins of a fort abandoned on the wind-scoured plains. What one feels in such places is, of course, the weighty impress of humanity.

In New Mexico, that humanity has been wildly assorted and, always, deeply individualistic. For all that has been made of the state's tri-cultural mix, those who look here for the exemplary melting pot will be disappointed. Indians, Hispanics and Anglos (and here, you will be told, a Chinese is an Anglo, a black is an Anglo, anyone not Indian or Spanish-American is an Anglo) all have clung to their traditions with an unprecedented tenacity. At worst, this has given rise to a racial animosity that even such a lofty and impartial source as the *Encyclopaedia Britannica* terms "the greatest single problem that New Mexico faces" (the E.B. then goes on, rather schoolmarmishly, to recommend "an atmosphere of trust and goodwill on all sides"). In this way, certainly, the state reflects a nation mired in the same terrible, age-old error.

At best, however, the side-by-side existence of three such strong ethnic entities provides the spice of New Mexican life; it has been suggested that, rather than a melting pot, the state is one big cultural stewpot, each group adding its own distinctive pungency to the heady mix, with no single flavor overwhelming another. Anthropologist Nancie L. Gonzalez (herself of Spanish-American descent) has written movingly about what she calls "a true pluralism": several cultures coexisting within the same society, "equal in terms of material welfare, self-determination, and role in government, but each retaining its individuality and self-pride." If such a dream can be achieved in this country, surely New Mexico must lead the way.

In writing this book, I join the legion of writers who have, over many years, paid tribute to New Mexico. I would particularly like to acknowledge (and urge readers to discover) the beautiful work of Oliver La Farge, Claire Morrill, Peggy Pond Church, Ross Calvin, John Nichols and Larry McMurtry (whose place is Texas, but whose heart occasionally has strayed over the border). Geologist Halka Chronic and historians Marc Simmons and David Lavender have provided both inspiration and hard fact.

I would also like to thank Mark Thompson, who took a flyer on an unknown quantity; and, always and for everything, Jeff, Anna and Daniel.

This book is for my mother, who gave me New Mexico.

STEPHEN TRIMBLE

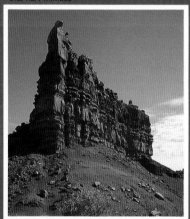

KENT KRONE

Top: A santo, *portrayal of San Miguel, on a* retablo *from the collections of Museum of New Mexico, Santa Fe.*
Above: Wind-sculpted red rock near Abiquiu.
Facing page: San Francisco de Asis mission church, Ranchos de Taos.

5

THE LAND

CHAPTER ONE

DENNIS & MARIA HENRY

Above: *Desert-dwelling scorpion.*

Facing page: *Stormlight over Bisti Badlands.*

If you love New Mexico, you may often find yourself struggling to convince the uninitiated that the state is more than just another section of Sunbelt, that it offers hidden, potent and extraordinarily diverse charms. "Well, the architecture is nice," the unbelievers might admit, simultaneously throwing passion a bone and acknowledging the pervasive influence of so-called "Santa Fe style." A compliment may be tendered to the cuisine (spicy!), the climate (sunny!), the crafts (special!). But mention the landscape, and bafflement reigns. "What's to love?" they cry. "It's all desert—and so flat!"

To be sure, there is some truth to this notion; New Mexico does encompass some of the flattest land in the world. But it also sports chain after rugged chain of mountains, some soaring more than two miles above sea level. There are, indeed, deserts in New Mexico: broiling badlands where even a cactus must struggle to survive. But there are also cool pine forests, lush meadows, fast-flowing streams stuffed with trout. In fact, the state's topography is as varied as the stewpot of its culture.

Big and almost square in shape (running 352 miles east-west and 391 miles north-south), New Mexico is bounded on the north by the mountains of Colorado, on the east by the panhandles of Oklahoma and Texas, on the south by Texas and the Mexican state of Chihuahua, and on the west by Arizona, which from 1850 to 1863 was part of the Territory of New Mexico. In the northwest, the state joins Arizona, Utah and Colorado at Four Corners, the only four-way meeting of states in the U.S., and the spot where everybody piles out of the car, vying for the opportunity to be photographed straddling four states at once.

New Mexico's land surface is divided into four geological provinces: Plains, Mountain, Plateau, and Basin and Range.

The Plains Province, covering the eastern third of the state, is an extension of the Great Plains, the western edge of the North American lowland. In the northerly section of this province lies (in Conrad Richter's phrase) a sea of grass. Early explorers reported that these prairies were shaggy with grasses growing higher than their saddle horns; because of grazing and development (some would say over-grazing and over-development), the tall grasses are a rare sight today. Farther south, between the Pecos and Canadian rivers, is the romantically named Llano Estacado, the Staked Plains, painfully flat and far from romantic to look at, but rich for both ranchers and wildcatters.

The Mountain Province sweeps through north-central New Mexico like a ridged backbone, tapering out just south of the state capital, Santa Fe. Its high and rugged peaks belong to the Sangre de Cristo (Blood of Christ) range, named for the red glow cast on their snowy reaches by the setting sun. The Sangres are the tail-end of the Rocky Mountains, a monumental range's last salute to the continent. The highest point in the state is here: 13,160-foot Wheeler Peak, near Taos (the lowest is Red Bluff, on the Pecos, at 2,817 feet).

Across the San Juan Mountains, to the west, lies the Plateau Province, part of the massive Colorado Plateau shared by New Mexico, Colorado, Arizona and Utah. High, generally level land intercut by deep canyons and studded with mesas, it often offers a red-rocked landscape, dramatic and—in a literal sense—colorful. This is the ancestral home of most of the Indian civilizations of the Southwest; Navajo, Zuni, Laguna and Acoma Indians have their reservations and pueblos here today.

Basin and Range is New Mexico's largest province, home to most of the state's population. A collection of stunningly-

6

TOM TILL

DENNIS & MARIA HENRY PHOTOS BOTH PAGES

Aspen glowing gold, early fall.

sweeping advance and sudden retreat of seas, of exploding volcanoes and encroaching deserts. But for all its drama, this is a story that is still being pieced together; the record of geologic events in New Mexico is fragmentary. Of the state's Precambrian history—a period beginning more than 2 billion years ago—particularly little is known. Precambrian rocks such as gneiss (a banded rock thought to form from granite or sandstone), schist (a flaky, mica-filled rock) and some sedimentary rocks (formed from particles of other rock deposited by water, wind or ice) are only rarely exposed in the mountain ranges that cluster in the western two thirds of the state. These rocks are metamorphic—formed from older rocks by great heat and pressure—and as such tell us that in Precambrian times, ancient New Mexico, although swept by seas, also was home to numerous volcanoes. Over and over again, tremendous volcanic explosions left the land veiled with volcanic ash. At the same time, the eroding forces of wind and rain were at work; around 1.35 billion years ago, after millions of years of erosion, only the roots of the original mountains remained.

But the process was far from over. In a new round of mountain-building, masses of molten rock—magma—spewed from the earth, eventually cooling into slabs of pink-red granite. Then, once again, erosion held sway; for more millions of years, New Mexico was flat and clean as a new slate, a trackless plain sloping toward a distant western sea.

For much of the Paleozoic Era (the Age of Fishes), North America was part of a megacontinent, Pangaea, which also included Europe, Asia, Africa and Antarctica. Some 570 million years ago, the western section of Pangaea tilted, allowing a sea to flow across it, depositing a succession of sedimentary rocks thick with marine fossils. Rock of this type is exposed throughout the mountains of New Mexico's Basin and Range Province, alternating with deposits of continental rock, lighter in color and density than that formed in ocean basins; the Sacramento Range is particularly rich with this distinctive, multi-hued layering.

In the late Paleozoic Era, a group of new mountains rose in north-central New Mexico, the tag-end of the ancestral Rocky Mountains stretching north into Colorado along the same general line as the present-day Rockies. Farther south, a great barrier reef had developed in bays lapping a shore

shaped mountain ranges separated by broad, dry basins, it stretches across the southwestern, central and south-central portions of the state. Its most important basins are the Rio Grande Valley, the Estancia Basin, the Tularosa Basin and the Plains of San Agustin; an attenuated roll call of its many ranges would include the Sandias and Manzanos crowding the Rio Grande Valley east of Albuquerque, the San Mateos to the west of Socorro, the San Andres snaking between Socorro and Las Cruces, the Sacramentos looming over Alamogordo, and the Mogollons to the southwest.

Mixed in with this already extraordinary variety of land forms are acres of pure-white gypsum sand dunes, roiling black lava flows, towering cinder cones, massive sunken calderas, limestone caverns extending to as-yet-unexplored depths, all attesting to a geologic history that has been, and continues to be, a drama—and a turbulent one, at that.

It is a story of reiterated mountain building, of the

along the site of today's New Mexico-Texas border. This was gradually cut off from the sea; as its water evaporated, vast deposits of salt, gypsum and potash were left behind, the origins of the remarkable dunes at White Sands, as well as the source of some of the state's most continuously productive mines.

The Mesozoic Era (the Age of Reptiles, from 245 million to 66 million years ago) saw continental sediments being deposited around new mountain ranges, forming the splashy red and pink rock formations that brighten the northwestern part of the state. Alluvial fans of gravel and sand—and flood plains of sand and silt—developed, while more violent volcanoes added further layers of volcanic ash to the landscape. Far to the west, the ancestral Sierra Nevada rose, cutting New Mexico off from the drift of Pacific moisture, allowing the land to grow dry.

It is this dryness that has helped to preserve some of the more arresting paleontological finds in the Southwest. This was the age of reptiles, after all, and dinosaurs roamed the earth, frequently finding themselves quite at home in New Mexico. One of the earliest dinosaurs, *Coelophysis,* evidently wandered over the northern part of the state in herds. More than a thousand specimens of the small, swift, carnivorous beast have been found near Ghost Ranch, Abiquiu, an area more recently hospitable to renowned painter Georgia O'Keeffe. Other important finds include a large *Camarasaurus,* excavated in 1978-1980 from Jurassic-period rock near San Ysidro in the Jemez Mountains; and more than 500 dinosaur footprints scattered over a mere two acres of Cretaceous-period sandstone in what is now Clayton Lake State Park, near New Mexico's far northeastern corner.

In the late Mesozoic Era, somewhere around 66 million years ago, the dinosaurs abruptly became extinct, along with about three-quarters of all plant and animal species then existing. There is still considerable debate among experts about why this happened, but a clue may be found in what geologists call the Cretaceous-Tertiary Boundary, the dividing line between the last period of the Age of Reptiles and the first period of the Age of Mammals: the time when dinosaurs and so many other plant and animal forms rushed to extinction. In many areas of the world—including the cliffs and slopes around Raton in northeast New Mexico—the Creta-

ceous-Tertiary Boundary is marked by a narrow layer of shale composed largely of iridium, an element rarely found on earth, but plentiful in meteorites. Scientists theorize that a series of enormous meteorite showers may have struck the earth, raising so much dust that the sun was effectively blotted out, perhaps for a period of years. With their environment abruptly rendered dark and freezing, plants would have died rapidly, followed in order by plant-eaters, meat-eaters, and finally, by the scavengers. Geologist Halka Chronic points out that just such a scenario is described by scientists who talk about the possible aftermath of a nuclear war, the aptly named "nuclear winter."

At the end of Mesozoic time, North America broke away from Europe, moving west; as the Cenozoic Era (the Age of Mammals) opened, the rift between the continents widened

Above: *Cast of a dinosaur footprint, one of hundreds found at Clayton Lake State Park.*
Left: *Erosion-carved arroyo.*

Angel Peak hovering over multi-hued sedimentary rock of Naci-miento Badlands, northwestern New Mexico.

some distant point in the future, the Rift may widen, ultimately splitting the continent apart to encompass a new sea. For now, the Rift contains the Rio Grande, a river that didn't have to carve its channel, but found one ready-made.

The same kind of violent faulting that created the Rio Grande Rift also gave rise to such distinctive elements of the New Mexican landscape as the brilliantly colored, stair-step plateaus of the northwest; pull-apart or tension faults farther east established the tilted mountains and deep basins of the Basin and Range Province. At the same time, intense volcanism along the western edge of the Rio Grande Rift scattered ash not only over New Mexico, but across the adjacent states as well. Many of these volcanoes finally collapsed, leaving sunken calderas, most notably the Jemez Caldera in the state's northwest—a vast, sun-scoured, surprisingly pastoral remnant of a violent past.

The Ice Ages that affected so much of North America and Europe had a slighter impact on New Mexico; there was no major glaciation over the state, although some small mountain glaciers did develop in the Sangre de Cristo and Brazos mountains. However, although the great glaciers did not extend their icy fingers so far south, their presence was felt in New Mexico in the form of a greatly increased rate of precipitation. As massive amounts of rain and snow drenched the state, lakes were born in the closed valleys of the south. The Rio Grande, originally a collection of small rivers and streams, often choked off in dead-end basins along the Rift, saw its many braided channels join forces to become a large, through-flowing river carrying water from the Colorado Rockies to the Gulf of Mexico. Floods became frequent, erosion increased and huge alluvial fans built up along the edges of various river valleys. The state's streams and rivers alternately deposited and wore down through layers of sand, gravel and silt. The results of much of this work may be seen today in the deeply-cut gorges and canyons so characteristic, in particular, of the northwestern and north-central parts of the state.

By about a million years ago, most of New Mexico's landscape looked much as it does today; the stage was set, ready for the extraordinary human pageant about to unfold. Scenery, however, would not be the only influence on the drama, not even scenery as obviously deterministic as the

into the Atlantic Basin. This westward movement of the continent has gone on for the last 66 million years—and continues today. During the initial shift, as the land broke open, the modern Rockies rose in almost the same position as their Paleozoic ancestors. A further by-product of the move was the development, some 30 million years ago, of two faults, enormous fractures in the earth cutting north-south down the length of New Mexico. Between the two deep but irregular faults, the earth's crust dropped down thousands of feet, creating the Rio Grande Rift, a vast valley-like formation similar to Africa's Great Rift. The Rio Grande Rift begins as a narrow slice in central Colorado, fanning out as it moves down through New Mexico: at Albuquerque, it is some 30 miles wide, while farther south, it is broad enough to contain the Rio Grande Valley, the badlands of the Jornada del Muerto, and the Tularosa Basin. Movement along the Rift's two encompassing faults continues today, suggesting that at isolating mountain ranges and endless plains. There were also special effects to consider: weather and its vital concomitant, water.

New Mexico's weather, as naturalist Haniel Long has noted, is "more independent"; this may, in fact, be the state that gave rise to the old saw that only fools and tenderfeet predict the weather. The climate may generally be called moderate; the mean annual temperature is 53° Fahrenheit. But extremes ranging from 29° below zero to 110° in the shade have been recorded, and it is not uncommon to see temperatures over a single day varying by as much as 40°. Again, the sun shines 70 percent of the year, making the state a leader in solar-energy research and application. This does not mean, however, that you can count on sun at any given moment; rapid turns and transformations are typical.

I remember a July day I spent wandering through Santa Fe. From morning to mid-afternoon, it was hot but comfortably dry. Abruptly, around three o'clock, the humidity rose to tropical proportions; my clothing fairly steamed. Big blue-and-silver clouds began to roll in from the Jemez Mountains, thunder rumbling ominously overhead. Within moments, the clouds split open and a torrent of rain flooded down; I was instantly as drenched as if I'd jumped into a pool fully dressed. I made a run for my hotel, just a few blocks away; before I got halfway there, the rain had changed to hail, and I found myself wincing under the onslaught of icy stones. Back at the hotel, I was able to look out at the churchyard of the Loretto Chapel: it was carpeted with white, the perfect picture of Christmas in July. I was astounded; natives shrugged.

So although this is a land where sunshine can be viewed as an exploitable resource (Albuquerque, for example, makes much of the fact that it suffers, on average, only five days a year of complete overcast), it is also a place where the wary will never wander into even the dryest-looking of arroyos, on even the most cloudless of days. Every summer, the local papers tell far too many tales of lives lost to flash floods; that these lost lives are usually those of non-natives is significant—and cautionary.

Electrical storms, too, seem to take on an added violence in these climes. Santa Fe is said to attract more wild lightning storms than anywhere else outside the Gulf Coast, stimulated by the hot air blowing up the sides of the mountains from the south and west. And out on the plains, I have witnessed two storms thundering toward each other from opposite points on the bowl of the horizon, finally merging to form one towering mass of blue cloud lit with green streaks of lightning.

Dust storms also may whip up out of nowhere, particularly during the summer months, when the earth is dry and the hot winds blow in from Mexico. They begin with ground streams; as wind velocity increases, the dust may rise as high as 12,000 feet. But perhaps most dreaded of all are the so-called "dry" storms: drifts of rain accompanied by thunder that blow away before they ever reach the ground. These are the worst because they are a tantalizing reminder of what New Mexico so badly needs and so rarely gets: water.

The fifth-largest state in the Union, New Mexico has an area of 121,666 square miles—but only about 250 square miles of surface water. Moreover, its replenishing rainfall is very unequally distributed: the upper reaches of the Sangre de Cristos may get 40 inches per annum, with other mountain ranges also catching rain in higher-than-average amounts; the eastern plains and high plateaus may do moderately well, receiving anywhere between 12 and 15 inches of rain; but the rest of the state (including much of the Rio Grande Valley) often records fewer than 10 inches of rain per year, very nearly qualifying as true desert.

How, then, have people survived in this (to borrow Mary Austin's phrase) "land of little rain"? First, New Mexico's rivers have supported life by making crop irrigation possible; agriculture has existed in their floodplains from prehistoric times. The Rio Grande, of course, has been the state's principal lifeline (see page 12), but although the state's other principal rivers may not match El Grande's legendary character, they, too, have played their part in New Mexico's history, commerce and sustenance.

From its headwaters in the lower fringes of the Sangre de Cristos, the Pecos River courses down to western Texas, its waters turning more and more alkaline the farther south it runs. But despite its infamous bitterness ("Her heart's as bitter as the Pecos" and other similar locutions were evidently common phraseology in the Old West), the Pecos has managed to sustain many cattle ranches and irrigate numerous farms in a region otherwise notoriously harsh and sere.

TOM BEAN

Towering, flat-bottomed cumulus clouds hold the promise of precious rain.

THE RIO GRANDE

STEPHEN TRIMBLE

One of the great rivers of the world, the fifth-longest river in North America, and so historically legendary as to dazzle the imagination, the Rio Grande has its headwaters in the Colorado Rockies, on the eastern face of the Continental Divide; it then courses south through New Mexico, Texas and Mexico (where it is known as the Rio Bravo); and finally empties into the Gulf of Mexico, after a journey of some 1,885 miles.

Four hundred seventy of those miles are New Mexican; the Rio Grande barrels north to south through the entire state, effectively cutting it in two. Initially, the river is imprisoned between the dark rock walls of a narrow basalt chasm; just north of Taos, this chasm is formally named the Rio Grande Gorge, its white rapids tumbling over black boulders designated the first Wild Rivers Recreation Area in the nation. Formed by erosion—the river cutting deeper as the volcanic plateau of Taos Mesa rose higher—the gorge is a 650-foot-deep gash in the level tableland. Riders, motorists, even the unwary walker—all have been known, at times, to plummet blindly over the edge, so little indication is there that the earth is about to crack open.

Farther south, the Rio Grande drops into the open terrain of the Basin and Range Province, flowing down along the pre-established line of the Rio Grande Rift. Its waters already have changed color from the crystalline blue of its source to the jade green frothed with white of the gorge region; once the vast valley of the rift is reached, the river turns brown with silt, a bolt of tan satin running shallow and slow. In these more arid regions, the Rio Grande does not carry a great volume of water; in some spots, year after year, it barely flows; on occasion, it goes dry.

Nevertheless, it has been, since prehistoric times, what it continues to be today: the focal point for New Mexico's development. The Anasazi, ancestors of the Pueblo Indians, made their way to its banks, establishing busy settlements more than a thousand years ago; the river made possible the subsistence farming—the crops of beans and corn—that supported them. When the Spanish began their drive north from Cortez's Mexico, the Rio Grande became their principal route for exploration and conquest; at a time when Boston was a bog, the capital city of Santa Fe already had been established near the river's edge. And when Americans began to pour into the New Mexican Territory, they immediately saw the river as a rich stream of commerce; the Spaniards may have been the first to explore the Rio Grande, but the pragmatic Anglos were the first to survey it scientifically.

Pragmatism is, perhaps, one approach to the river today. New Mexico has, in recent years, prudently established several water treaties relating to the use of the Rio Grande, including the Rio Grande Compact (1939) with Colorado and Texas, concerning shared use of the waters of the Upper Rio Grande sub-basin (above the site of the former Fort Quitman, Texas), and the Pecos River Compact (1948) with Texas, detailing the use of the Pecos (a major tributary of the Rio Grande) above Girvin, Texas. A reservoir with several million acre-feet of storage capacity has been established at Elephant Butte (a startling show of sparkling waters, almost a mirage hovering in the bone-dry badlands between two shaggy mountain ranges).

And while irrigation is still the river's principal use, its waters now generate considerable hydroelectric power—the perfect complement to the energy expended by those who look on the river as one long recreational paradise.

Still, however pragmatic one is forced to be in this day and age, it seems possible that the Rio Grande's greatest legacy is, quite simply, its legend. It is, truly, a great river, able to evoke shining images of a highly colored past in a slow flow of brown water. Stand on its banks in the shade of a fluttering cottonwood, under the molten gold of an autumn aspen; look out across the narrow reach of water to the pink and purple mesas backed by the blue of a distant mountain range. The pageant unreels: the Ancient Ones, quietly worshipping the natural world; conquistadors, splendid horses prancing, armor glinting in the sun; mountain men, shrewdly trapping and trad-

"The Box," Rio Grande Wild River Recreation Area, near Taos.

ing their way to the top of frontier society. The river is timeless; New Mexico's past, present and future run together in its braided streams.

DENNIS & MARIA HENRY

The hardy juniper, denizen of New Mexico's Upper Sonoran life zone.

The Canadian River, also originating from a group of streams in the Sangre de Cristos, flows east toward the Texas Panhandle. It, too, was infamous in the days of early settlement; to go north of the Canadian was to enter unknown, uncharted territory, rife with hazard. Appropriately, the river was named for a handful of enterprising French Canadian traders who found their way into New Mexico in 1739 from French bases along the Mississippi, thereby flabbergasting the Spanish.

New Mexico's other major river, the San Juan, is a tributary of the Colorado River. Although it barely arcs across the extreme northeast corner of the state, it nevertheless carries some 70 percent of the surface water available in New Mexico for urban use; without the waters of the San Juan, Albuquerque might not be the booming metropolis it is today.

The conservation and effective use of what little water exists has, historically, been of vital importance to New Mexico. The Pueblo Indians and the Hispanic settlers who followed utilized even the smallest streams, establishing communities wherever dependable sources of water could be found, learning to master the art of irrigation. In this century,

13

DENNIS & MARIA HENRY PHOTOS BOTH PAGES

Casting for trout on the San Juan River, northwestern New Mexico.

experts confidently foresee plentiful moisture for years to come, while others predict that the supply will be utterly tapped out in the not-too-distant future. There are those who look on the latter possibility as a blessing in disguise for New Mexico, and certainly it is a potent argument against growth: where there are inadequate supplies of water, how can anyone lobby for development?

Meanwhile, even with abundantly flowing ground water, New Mexico exists in a condition that experts call "moisture deficiency," sometimes exceeding 20 inches. This means that no matter how rich the alluvial soil or how beneficent the temperate climate, unless 20 or more inches of irrigation water are provided at regular intervals, crops will not grow. Under such dire conditions, is it any wonder that water has taken on sociological, political, even mythic significance for New Mexicans? Haniel Long has noted that there is more space in the daily paper devoted to water and related issues than to any other single subject. It is not uncommon to hear about crimes of violence committed over some violation of water rights; nor is it unusual for the perpetrators to be acquitted, the general feeling being that any man who'd mess with another man's water pretty much deserves what he gets. By consensus, one of the most important men in each New Mexican community is the official in charge of the local *acequia*, or communal irrigation ditch. And it is certainly no accident that the key incident in the most famous work of modern New Mexican fiction, John Nichols' *The Milagro Beanfield War*, is an act not of fornication or assassination or even revolution, but of irrigation.

Each spring, as New Mexicans lucky enough to live along an acequia devote their energies to cleaning out their sections of ditch (those who don't must pay a fine to the ditch boss), various deities are offered thanks for the newly flowing water. They might just as logically be thanked for the mountains, whose soaring peaks are the true instruments of New Mexico's salvation. Without its mountains, the entire state would be a desert, scoured by the scorching drafts blowing inward from the Gulf of California and the Pacific on one side, and from the Gulf of Mexico on the other. Fortunately, the state's many ranges force the hot winds to rise and, at higher altitudes, let go of their moisture.

Under certain circumstances, mountains also can have

dams and flood-control projects on the Pecos have made farming possible on thousands of heretofore undeveloped acres near Carlsbad and Roswell, while, since 1940, the Conchas Dam on the Canadian has provided water to irrigate land near Tucumcari, thus giving birth to a newly productive agricultural area.

But such efforts are not always successful; irrigation efforts along the San Juan, for example, have proved relatively unworkable. Moreover, the state is susceptible—like the rest of the Southwest—to severe periodic droughts, which render even such water sources as the mighty Rio Grande unreliable. As a result, New Mexicans have come to rely increasingly on the series of aquifers and underground lakes that underlies much of the south-central part of the state. This subterranean water system is formed by the slow seepage of mountain runoff through porous soils; many natural springs and artesian wells tap into it, providing more than half the state's irrigation water.

With dependence on ground water growing by leaps and bounds, the critical question becomes: how renewable is this resource? Unfortunately, there is no clearcut answer; some the opposite effect, draining clouds at their summits but creating what are called "rain shadows," leaving the valleys and basins on their lee sides dry. The ring of towering mountains around the Colorado Plateau, for example, make it one of the driest parts of the Southwest, despite its high elevation. But by and large, an increase in elevation means, as has been noted, an increase in precipitation.

The fact that New Mexico is a state of generally high elevation (remember that its lowest point is nearly 3,000 feet above sea level) also affects its average temperature, making it cooler than other areas at the same latitude; temperatures tend to rise or fall five degrees with every thousand feet of elevation. Altitude has also made it possible for the state to support six of the seven life zones (all but the tropical), with their many varieties of flora and fauna.

The Lower Sonoran Zone, usually established at altitudes of less than 4,500 feet, embraces the southern sections of the Rio Grande and Pecos valleys, as well as the state's southwestern corner. This is the land generally referred to as "desert," and it is home to the more exotic plants: scrubby creosote, named for the pungent smell of its yellow-green leaves; thorny mesquite, with its edible seed pods and enormous tap roots; and such other prickly items as yuccas, cacti, agaves and ocotillos. In spite of its inhospitable appearance, however, this zone includes nearly 20,000 square miles of New Mexico's best grazing and irrigated farmland.

The Upper Sonoran Zone covers some three quarters of the state, including most of the plains, foothills and valleys above 4,500 feet. Many varieties of prairie grasses grow here, but perhaps the most characteristic vegetation are the fragrant piñon trees (see page 17) and juniper shrubs. Dwarfish at the lower reaches of the Zone, piñon and juniper grow both taller and thicker at higher altitudes, thanks to a greater annual rainfall.

The Transition Zone, covering some 19,000 square miles of the state, is composed primarily of large stands of ponderosa pine; the Canadian Zone consists of around 4,000 square miles of blue spruce and Douglas fir, while the Hudsonian and Arctic-Alpine zones, at the rarefied altitudes above 9,500 feet, are small in area and sparsely covered by vegetation, presenting their rocky domes baldly to the sky.

Most of New Mexico's almost 10 million acres of na-

tional forest land are located in these mid- to upper-altitude zones, managed by the USDA Forest Service as "a multiple-use resource for timber, water, minerals, wildlife, vegetation and recreational activities." Similarly, the Bureau of Land Management administers another 13 million acres of public lands throughout the state, with the goal of "providing benefits from recreation, range, timber, minerals, oil and gas, watershed, fish and wildlife, wilderness and natural scenic, scientific and cultural values."

Unfortunately, the stated goals of the Forest Service and the BLM have, on occasion, come into conflict with the needs of New Mexicans. Small-scale ranchers—Hispanic sheepmen, in particular—argue that larger operations, often run by out-of-state conglomerates, are consistently favored by federal agencies in the matter of grazing rights on public lands. The situation is exacerbated by the fact that many of these lands belonged, until this century, to the ancestors of the sheepmen. Perhaps even more painful was the 50-year struggle of the Taos Indians to wrest Blue Lake—their sacred site for a millenium—back from the Forest Service, which had appropriated it for the Carson National Forest. The Taoseños' ultimate victory in 1971 was more emblematic of their courage and tenacity than of any sudden enlightenment on the part of the Forest Service.

No one will deny, however, the Forest Service's zeal for protecting New Mexico's diverse wildlife. In this, the Service has been aided by the relative inaccessibility of much of the state; the wall-like mountain ranges and forbiddingly dry plains that made New Mexico slow to yield to human settlement also have helped to preserve an abundance of animal life.

Fossilized remains of a great variety of mammals have been found throughout the state, bearing mute testimony to the evolution of horses and camels (which found their way, via land bridge, to Asia and Europe, the camels never returning, the horses not until brought back by Coronado and his soldiers), wild dogs, large cats, bears and many species with no modern descendants. Today, mountain and forest areas above 7,000 feet are home to deer, brown bear, mink, muskrat, fox, mountain lion and beaver, the animal whose luxuriant pelt brought many of the first mountain men (trappers, by trade) to the area. The plains play host to antelope, coyote, prairie

Sheep graze the irrigated plains near Portales.

15

DENNIS & MARIA HENRY PHOTOS

Above: Mule deer buck.

Right: Mexican wolf, object of intensive state and federal preservation programs.

dog and jack rabbit, while the more desert-like regions are lands of lizards, snakes, scorpions, spiders and the state bird, the personable roadrunner.

New Mexico's mountain streams can boast of many species of trout; warm-water fish abound in lower streams. The state operates six trout hatcheries, and the distribution, ecology and life history of trout and other game fish are being investigated on a continuing basis by state fisheries biologists. Of special note is the Department of Game and Fish's program to promote the development of kokanee salmon; in 1987, more than a million salmon eggs were harvested and planted in state waters.

A total of 23 fishes are on the Department of Game and Fish's list of endangered species, joining—at last count—14 mammals, 30 birds, 16 reptiles, five amphibians, 19 mollusks and one crustacean. These species are the subject of frequent inventories, counts, surveys and investigations. State person-

nel have participated in federal recovery programs designed to preserve such animals as the Mexican wolf, the southern Rocky Mountain/Southwest peregrine falcon and a variety of desert fishes. Special operations are now in effect to study and preserve mule deer, bobcats and Merriam's turkeys, among others. Intensive care has been extended to the state's populations of desert bighorn sheep and Rocky Mountain bighorn sheep, with the aim of eliminating certain endemic diseases and reintroducing the animals where they have died out.

A particular effort has been made to preserve the endangered species among the state's 300 species of birds; several national wildlife refuges are managed to provide them with food, shelter and water. The prairie chicken (a type of grouse) has made a spectacular recovery from near-extinction at several preserves in the eastern part of the state. Sandhill cranes, quail and pheasant may be seen at the Bitter Lake National Wildlife Refuge near Roswell; whooping cranes, sandhill cranes and snow geese at the Bosque del Apache Refuge near San Antonio; and raptors such as prairie and peregrine falcons, golden and bald eagles, rough-legged and Swainson's hawks, burrowing owls and kestrels at the Las Vegas National Wildlife Refuge outside Las Vegas.

These lists of birds and fishes, delicate antelope and lumbering bear, scuttling creatures of the desert and shy inhabitants of mountain heights—they are rich with life, appropriate partners to the vast and varied landscape of New Mexico. It seems only fitting, then, that the flood of history soon to engulf such a vivid natural panorama should be equally various, equally tumultuous, equally teeming with life. And it was.

THE PIÑON

DENNIS & MARIA HENRY

STEPHEN TRIMBLE

Although much has been made of New Mexico's extraordinary light and wine-like air, not enough has been said, in this writer's opinion, about its exquisite and characteristic fragrance: the haunting, sweetly smoky scent of burning piñon wood. On a frosty night, with the smoke from a thousand fires rising to perfume the chilled air, the effect is equal to any melange of magnolias or orange blossoms—better, because of its woodsy, slightly astringent quality.

The tree that provides New Mexico's fragrant fuel is the unpromising looking piñon pine *(pinus edulis)*, the twisted, scrubby little tree scattered over so much of the state's Upper Sonoran life zone. Dark green, with small, rust-colored cones, the piñon is proficient at leeching moisture from the region's drier soils; at the same time, its tenacious root system helps to prevent erosion. But the tree's greatest treasure is revealed each fall, usually after the first frost, when its mature cones open, revealing its seeds—piñon nuts.

For thousands of years, the inhabitants of New Mexico have been harvesting the tiny edible nut. The earliest Spanish explorers found Native Americans gathering them; Coronado mentioned them in 1540. The Navajos made them a major trading crop in their dealings with other tribes, and even today still gather them for commercial purposes. The oldest and simplest method of harvesting has been to simply gather the nuts where they fell on the ground; it has been said that a fast worker, using this technique, can pick up to 20 pounds of nuts a day. Often, the harvest is a family affair, kids spreading sheets under the trees to catch the nuts their elders beat down with sticks.

Piñon nuts require two years to mature; according to various folklores, a particularly heavy crop comes along every third, fifth or seventh year. Although the nuts are a cash crop (four fifths of which is sold outside the state), supply continues to exceed demand. This may not be the case for long, since it is now recognized that piñons are both excellent keepers—unshelled, they stay good for up to three years if kept dry—and exceptionally nutritious, being higher in protein and carbohydrates but lower in fat than (for comparison's sake) pecans.

Above: A sturdily sculptural piñon.
Inset: Piñon nuts.

And they are delicious, in everything from a good garlicky pesto sauce to a sticky-sweet confection locally dubbed "piñon-uche." There are those, however, who prefer to keep things simple, and like nothing better than a snack of raw shelled piñon nuts consumed while basking in the fragrant warmth of a piñon wood fire.

THE PEOPLE

JONATHAN A. MEYERS

Above: Fibrolite ax heads, circa 1550-1672, found at Gran Quivira Pueblo ruins, Salinas National Monument.

Facing page: Corn—the mainstay crop of the Pueblos, both ancient and modern— stands side by side with sunflowers at Pecos National Monument.

One clear, dry day in 1908, George McJunkin, a cowboy and former slave, was riding up Wild Horse Gulch, an arroyo near the little village of Folsom in New Mexico's northeast corner. As he rode, something caught McJunkin's keen eye: protruding from the dusty walls of the gulch were dozens of massive bleached bones. They were not, McJunkin immediately realized, the usual detritus of the range; he dismounted and went to investigate. To his astonishment, he found, scattered among the strange-looking bones, a large number of finely worked flint spear points, unlike anything he had ever seen.

Not until 1925, when archaeologists were finally persuaded to dig up the first Folsom site, did the full significance of McJunkin's discovery become clear. Then it was learned that the bones he had found were the remains of a herd of extinct giant bison, and that the spear points—hereafter renowned as Folsom points—belonged to men who had lived and hunted in North America during the Ice Age, 8,000 to 10,000 years ago. Subsequent discoveries—of spear points near Clovis and in Sandia Cave near Albuquerque—pushed the date of human occupation of New Mexico back still farther, to some 12,000 years ago.

These first New Mexicans were nomadic hunters, trailing mammoths, bison, antelope, giant sloths and early camels and horses. According to some theories, they followed the herds over a Siberian land bridge from Asia, slowly moving south over a period of many years. They came, finally, to a New Mexico very different than the one we know today, a cool wet paradise of thick forests and grassy savannas, rich with wild fruits and nuts, able to support herds of animals so enormous that to look down on them from the hills was to see an entire valley floor alive with movement.

Then, with the end of the Ice Age (around 8000 to 7000 B.C.), New Mexico's climate changed, growing dry; the grasslands withered. Game, their numbers already greatly reduced by hunting, could no longer survive; without meat, neither could the hunters. So they moved on—many, it has been suggested, to the Great Plains.

But the Western part of what would be New Mexico remained populated, most likely by an influx of new people. These were desert-dwellers, with a more varied diet—small game, seeds, roots—that was better adapted to the newly arid land. By 2,000 to 5,000 years ago, the people of this Desert Culture—known in their later developmental stages as the Cochise—had become at least part-time agrarians. Although still nomadic, journeying from place to place with the seasons and living in such natural shelters as caves and rock outcrops, they began to plant seeds, returning months later to harvest. Evidence for this revolutionary development has been found in such places as Bat Cave in western New Mexico: tiny ears of corn, only two to three inches long, dating from about 1000 B.C.

Most experts believe that this corn (and with it, the beginnings of agriculture) came from the south, from the more advanced peoples of Mexico. Other crops soon followed: beans, squash, melons, cotton. Crops were an anchor; gradually, the Cochise wanderers began to settle where they planted and harvested. And these settlers developed, in New Mexico, two distinct cultures.

First to blossom were the Mogollon, named for the mountains where their artifacts have been found in the southwestern part of the state. The Mogollon were aided by their proximity to Mexico, which provided them not only with crops, but also with one of the hallmarks of early

STEPHEN TRIMBLE

LIBRARY MEDIA CENTER
ALBUQUERQUE ACADEMY

GLENN VAN NIMWEGEN

Extraordinary Anasazi masonry endures at Pueblo del Arroyo, Chaco Canyon.

they raised pottery-making from a primitive craft to a high art. Weapons such as the atlatl and spear were displaced by the more efficient bow and arrow, borrowed, in all probability, from Plains Indians. This swift acceptance of new ways—and the subsequent improvement upon them—is characteristic of a people who can be described only as curious, adaptable and brilliant.

The most celebrated accomplishment of the Anasazi may be seen even today: the complex network of villages—pueblos—that lie, magnificent ruins, over the northwest quarter of the state. Rapidly developing their extraordinary skills as masons, the Anasazi carved and built multi-storied residences, kivas (the highly sacred underground ceremonial chambers) and plazas out of sheer rock: cities that have outlasted their makers by centuries. Chaco Canyon, Aztec Ruins, Frijoles Canyon, Puye: these (with Mesa Verde in Colorado and Kayenta in Arizona) were the L.A., Chicago and New York of the ancient Southwest—in many ways more successful, and certainly more beautiful.

From roughly 1100 to 1300 A.D., the Anasazi consolidated the rapid gains of the preceding centuries. The Classic Pueblo Period (named for the towns so finely hewn during this time) was a golden age, witness to the construction of the largest and most intricately designed pueblos. Chaco Canyon, for example, was a tiny valley barely a mile wide. Yet it eventually supported a population of some 7,000 people, suggesting a high degree of social organization, astonishingly efficient methods of farming and food procurement, and a level of personal civility unheard of in our own era: how else could Chacoans have lived in such close quarters with such evident amiability?

Beyond their singular gifts for city-building, the Anasazi also became the finest potters of their age, fashioning ollas (water jars), canteens, cups and vessels of all shapes and sizes, decorated with the exquisitely detailed black-and-white designs so admired today. They were talented jewelers and weavers, as well; they quarried stone; they mined turquoise, obsidian, hematite and salt; they traded with peoples all over the Southwest, and possibly as far west as the Pacific; they constructed reservoirs, dams and irrigation ditches; and they built a series of broad, straight roads emanating in a circular grid from Chaco Canyon that befuddle archaeologists (why

civilization: pottery. By around 300 B.C., the Mogollon were turning out primitive jars; by 500 A.D., they were the cultural leaders of the Southwest, living in villages of pit houses (round, shallow dwellings walled and roofed with mud-mortared timber), worshiping in large ceremonial lodges, cultivating many crops and producing burnished red and brown ceramic ware.

The Mogollon influence drifted north to the Four Corners area, to the people of the Colorado Plateau. These people, although still largely nomadic and not so culturally advanced as their neighbors to the south, made exceptional baskets, so tightly woven they could be used to carry water; they are known today as the Basket Makers. Within a mere few centuries, by the end of the first millenium A.D., they were to make an astounding cultural leap, evolving into one of the greatest—and certainly most mysterious—civilizations this continent ever has known. The Navajo later gave them the name by which we know them: Anasazi, the Ancient Ones.

Rapidly, the Anasazi gave up their wandering ways and became agriculturalists, in all likelihood improving upon methods that had been introduced from the south; similarly, did the horseless, cartless Anasazi need roads? were they trade routes? ceremonial? defensive?) and dazzle engineers. With all this, the greatest achievement of the Anasazi was their society as a whole: dynamic, but at the same time stable, solid, secure.

And yet, mysteriously, sometime in the 13th century, the Anasazi began to leave their homes. By 1300, the great cities of the Colorado Plateau were empty, wind-swept, already imprisoned in the silence of abandonment. There are several possible explanations for the abrupt departure. Tree-ring analysis indicates that a severe drought struck the Plateau region between 1276 and 1299; the Anasazi may have been starved out. Still, the same kind of study shows that they had survived earlier, equally severe droughts; and there is evidence that the exodus from the pueblos began before this dry spell. Other theories suggest that the migration may have been caused by internal dissension, epidemic disease or constant raids by marauding nomadic tribes. Probably, it was some combination of factors, but the Anasazi left no record, and the questions about their mysterious departure remain essentially unanswerable.

Drifting, the Anasazi moved south and east, some to the upper and middle Rio Grande regions, others either forming or joining communities at Zuni, Acoma and Laguna. Displaced, they found it difficult to maintain the glories of the past; architecture, arts and crafts declined. But agricultural pursuits persisted, as did trade and exchange of customs and ideas with the Plains Indians; by the 16th century, on the eve of the Spanish conquest, these ancestors of present-day Pueblo Indians were living comfortably in some 75 to 80 pueblos trailing from the Piro villages of the mid-Rio Grande Valley north to Taos and west to Zuni. Although they shared similar beliefs, skills and ways of living, these tribes were actually quite individual, separated principally by the fact that they did not share a language; even today, Indians of the 19 modern pueblos speak, variously, Zuni, Keresan and the Tiwa, Tewa and Towa dialects of the Tanoan tongue. It may be speculated that throughout the years of struggle with the Spanish, one thing that kept the Pueblos from a constructive unity was their lack of a common language; it also has kept them independent, in the best sense of the word.

Meanwhile, other tribes had begun to make their appearance on the high plains of eastern New Mexico. Coming

TOM BEAN

Ruins of Pueblo Bonito at Chaco Canyon show the importance of spiritual life for the Anasazi: each circular structure was a kiva, or ceremonial chamber.

originally from Canada, these loosely organized bands may have arrived in the Southwest as early as the 13th century; it has been suggested that their raids may have contributed to the abandonment of Anasazi homelands. Other experts place their arrival in New Mexico somewhere around 1500, just before the appearance of the Spanish. They were a motley group of clans and families related by the Athabascan language and by their fierce and nomadic ways: the Apache.

They soon scattered over a broad area, moving steadily on foot, their large, lupine dogs dragging travois packed with hide tipis, personal possessions, religious objects and the weapons required for raids or the hunt. The Apache de Navaju (today's Navajo) wandered across the Continental Divide, settling on the high plateau of New Mexico's northwest. The Navajo soon distinguished themselves from their Apache cousins, utilizing agrarian techniques learned from the Pueblo Indians; they retained a semi-nomadic existence, however, moving about with the seasons, building log and mud houses—hogans—in each place of settlement. The Jicarilla Apache (famous for their small baskets, or *jicarillas*) remained in the rugged country of the north-central region,

TOM TILL

west of the Rio Grande; like the Navajo, they traded with and learned farming from their Pueblo neighbors. The Mescaleros (named for their favored delicacy, the heart of the mescal plant) made their way into the beautiful Sacramento Mountains, to the southeast; while a fourth group, the Chiricahua, roamed southwestern New Mexico, eventually becoming known·as some of the most skilled warriors in the West.

The skills of war, however, were not yet the vital necessities they were soon to become. With the Pueblo Indians, the Apache and Navajo were developing a mutually beneficial relationship, adopting each other's customs, trading Apache buffalo hides and dried buffalo meat for Pueblo vegetables and pottery. But the sudden (and to the Indians, utterly astonishing) intrusion of the Spaniards into their ordered world would alter this relationship—and so much else— forever.

The saga of the Spanish conquest of New Mexico—and a saga it was, full of dramatic advances and perilous retreats, peopled by the greedy, the good and the glory-bound— properly begins in the spring of 1536, when four tattered, exhausted souls stumbled into the northern frontiers of New Spain (Mexico), the colony only recently wrested by Cortez from the Aztecs. They were three Spaniards and a Moorish slave, the only survivors of an expedition that had set sail for Florida eight years earlier. They had been shipwrecked, taken prisoner by coastal Indians, escaped, and then had spent literal years wandering on foot across Texas and probably through parts of New Mexico and Arizona, surviving among the Indians by acting as healers.

Their arrival in New Spain excited great interest not, paradoxically, because of the actual events of their extraordinary journey, but because of Spanish hopes for the unknown territory they had crossed. The little group's leader, Alvar Nunez Cabeza de Vaca, flatly described an impoverished land whose modest inhabitants could offer no more than turquoise and coral beads, a few arrowheads, and an occasional story about people far to the north who lived in large houses. It was the legend rather than the facts that caught the attention of Spanish officials. Couldn't the people to the north be, in fact, the inhabitants of the fabled cities of gold, the seven cities of Cibola?

The Viceroy of New Spain, Antonio de Mendoza, was

determined to find out. He tried to persuade Cabeza de Vaca and his confreres to guide an exploratory party north; they refused, so Mendoza promptly bought Esteban, the black slave who had accompanied them, and installed him as scout for a group of men led by Fray Marcos de Niza, a Franciscan priest who had travelled with Pizarro in Peru.

The expedition was a disaster. Fray Marcos ordered Esteban to ride ahead with a retinue of Indians, paving the way and making regular reports on his progress by sending back crosses: small ones to indicate finds of little value, large ones to announce truly splendid discoveries. As Fray Marcos and his company approached the Zuni village of Hawikuh (just inside the western border of modern New Mexico), a very large cross was delivered. Fray Marcos hurried forward, only to discover that Esteban had been slain by the Zuni.

Horrified, Fray Marcos beat a hasty retreat to New Spain, probably without ever seeing Zuni, although his defenders argue that he viewed it from a distance, the light from the setting sun washing it with a glow suspiciously, excitingly golden. In either case, the friar's insecure grasp of the facts did not prevent him from reporting to Mendoza that the pueblo was a glorious settlement of seven villages larger than Mexico City: Cibola itself! Mendoza immediately ordered a full-scale expedition to be led by a young provincial governor, Francisco Vasquez de Coronado; significantly, Coronado was a wealthy man who agreed to partially finance the expedition.

The elaborate party of 275 cavalrymen, half a hundred foot soldiers, a few wives and children, a thousand Indian slaves, 1,100 head of pack stock and hundreds of cattle, sheep and goats headed north on February 22, 1540. Six friars, including the fabulist Fray Marcos, also went along, a reminder of Mendoza's last injunction to Coronado: to Christianize the Indians he might meet, not slaughter them. At their head rode Coronado, resplendent in gilded armor and an elegantly plumed helmet.

Six months later, the weary crew, considerably less splendid, arrived at Hawikuh. They were greeted with showers of stones and responded brutally, with steel, explicitly going against Mendoza's orders and setting a tragic precedent for the next three centuries. Moreover, when the slaughter was over and they finally entered the Zuni town, they found not the glorious city of gold they had been led to expect, but a

MUSEUM OF NEW MEXICO

Above: Alvar Nunez Cabeza de Vaca and his little band—the first Spaniards to set foot in the Southwest—spent years wandering "the Great American Desert" before reaching Mexico to tell their story.

Facing page: Cottonwoods gleam gold over Aztec Ruins National Monument, northern New Mexico.

barely accoutred village built of mud. Fray Marcos, his perfidy or—at best—his unreliability revealed, was once again forced to flee south.

For another two years, Coronado was led across New Mexico, Texas, Oklahoma and finally into present-day Kansas in constant pursuit of the golden dream. Pueblo peoples, anxious to be rid of the brutal invaders, kept feeding him stories of greater, more gilded cities to the north; Coronado kept swallowing these tales of wealth. Finally, in 1542, he returned to New Spain, a self-confessed failure. In 1544, he was accused by the government of mismanagement of the expedition; convicted, fined and stripped of his office, he never recovered. Although his conviction was later reversed by a higher court, Coronado lived in painful obscurity until his death in 1556.

For some four decades after Coronado's disaster, the officials of New Spain were markedly reluctant to venture once more into the hostile lands to the north. But tales of riches kept filtering into eager ears; equally significant were the stories of countless souls to be saved among the heathen

Coronado's men attack the Zuni village of Hawikuh, 1540.

Indians. The phrase often used to describe the Spaniards was "For gold, God and glory"; that these goals were contradictory seems obvious, perhaps, only in hindsight.

By 1583, King Philip II of Spain had decided that the time was ripe for a new attempt at colonizing the northern territories. But it took 14 long years for the Viceroy of New Spain to find the right man for the job: Don Juan de Onate, son of a silver baron, related by marriage to both Cortez and the Aztec emperor Moctezuma, and a man accustomed to harsh command. As with Coronado, Onate's wealth was a key factor, for he essentially financed the expedition, to the tune of some $4 million in today's terms. In exchange, he was named civil governor of New Mexico, captain general of the provincial troops and *adelantado* ("he who goes first"), an honorary title of great significance to the Spaniards. He would further have the right to a land grant of his own choosing, to extend 30 square leagues—approximately three quarters of a million acres.

The colonists who headed north in January of 1598 included about 400 men, 130 of whom had brought along their wives and children. Ten friars accompanied them, as did several Tlascala Indians from central Mexico, impressed to do manual labor and to reassure tribes of the north who had never seen Europeans. With 83 carts and 7,000 head of livestock, the column stretched out for some four miles.

Cutting through a pass in the mountains (near what is today El Paso), they struck out up the Rio Grande. It seems, nearly 400 years later, horrifyingly appropriate that they almost immediately found themselves wandering across the barren stretch of badlands soon to be known as the Jornada del Muerto (Journey of the Dead). For their journey, a 10-year epic of struggle and error, was not to be a happy one.

Founding their capital, San Gabriel, north of present-day Espanola, the colonists then turned, not to a development of the lands available to them, but to a vain search for silver and gold. Once it became apparent that such riches were not going to materialize, the colonists became disillusioned, losing interest in the struggling little colony.

Meanwhile, relations with the Indians, initially cordial, had deteriorated. One of the more infamous episodes in the early life of New Mexico occurred when a group of Spaniards attempted to requisition food from the inhabitants of Acoma Pueblo, the beautiful "sky city" established on a mesa-top west of the Rio Grande. Agreeing to provide supplies, the Acoma people lured the Spaniards to their lofty stronghold, then fell upon them, killing 10, including Onate's favorite nephew. Onate responded mercilessly, sending a punitive force that left Acoma in ruins, and some 600 to 800 Indians massacred. The survivors—about 70 men and 500 women and children—were charged with murder and armed opposition to their "new masters." They were sentenced harshly: men and women alike to 20 years of slavery, with the additional proviso that all males over the age of 25 have one foot cut off. Sixty young girls were sent to convents in Mexico City, never to see their homeland or families again; children were handed over to the Franciscans; and two Hopis who had been visiting Acoma had their right hands amputated and were released, to serve as living reminders of Spanish wrath.

The harshest discipline was not enough to save the colony of New Mexico. Although Onate accomplished much in the way of exploration (one of his duties as governor of the province, but perhaps also a contributing factor in his downfall, since it required him to be away from the capital for months at a time), he had been a miserable failure as a colonizer, enduring countless desertions, accusations of criminal behavior, and charges of gross mismanagement. In 1607, Onate was recalled, and grimly started south for New Spain. With him was his 22-year-old son, to whom he had hoped to hand on the magnificent colony of his dreams; but as the party crossed the Jornada del Muerto, Indians attacked, killing one Spaniard—Onate's boy—and the last of his hopes. Like Coronado before him, he rode on to trial, a broken man.

The colony of New Mexico, meanwhile, hung by a thread, on the verge of being abandoned. But the King of Spain was persuaded to persevere by the Franciscans, who claimed 8,000 converts among the Pueblo Indians; these newly rescued souls could not, it was argued, be cut adrift. King Philip agreed; on November 1, 1609, he made New Mexico a royal colony under direct control of the crown, with Pedro de Peralta as its new governor. Peralta headed north with instructions to move the capital from San Gabriel to a more strategic site, one close enough to the Pueblos to keep a careful eye on them, yet far enough removed to avoid conflicts over land and water. He chose a site along a stream, not far from the Rio Grande and sheltered by the foothills of the Sangre de Cristos; there among the piñons, in a light of remarkable clarity, he founded Santa Fe, the City of the Holy Faith. Established in 1610, Santa Fe—not Boston, not Philadelphia, not any of the leafy Eastern towns—is the oldest capital city in the United States.

With the founding of the new capital, officials of both church and state plunged with renewed energy into the development of the New Mexican colony. What this meant, effectively, was a vigorous exploitation of the Pueblo peoples. Under the *encomienda* system, heads of Indian households were required to pay an annual tribute in corn and blankets to the Spaniards; similarly, a work levy, *repartimiento,* forced the Pueblos to labor for the Spaniards, tilling their fields and tending their livestock. The Franciscans, who might have been expected to defend their charges from such institutionalized slavery, were blinded by zeal: in their search for souls, they committed even more heinous crimes.

With virtually no understanding of the power of native

Gerald Cassidy's romanticized depiction (painted in 1921) of Coronado's ill-fated expedition to New Mexico.

religion, the friars forced the Pueblos to build churches and mission compounds, and worse, to worship in them. Failure to follow priestly orders was punished by flogging, time in the stocks or head-shaving, deeply humiliating for any Indian. Although many Indians went through the ceremonies of conversion, they nevertheless refused to give up their own religion; accordingly, the Franciscans stepped up their attacks, condemning native priests as sorcerers, raiding the sacred kivas, defiling altars, holding public burnings of masks, prayer plumes, fetishes and other holy articles, and banning ceremonial dances and displays.

The Pueblos were further ravaged by white men's diseases: smallpox, measles, whooping cough and cholera, hitherto unknown among Indians. Moreover, they were starving: a severe drought at the end of the 1660s made forced tributes, already a hardship, a form of genocide. The Apache, formerly

MUSEUM OF NEW MEXICO IMAGES BOTH PAGES

Above: Don Diego de Vargas recon- quered New Mexico a dozen years after the Pueblo Revolt of 1680 sent Spaniards retreating south.

Facing page: Don Juan Bautista de Anza, colonial governor of New Mexico 1778-1788, made peace with the Comanche, ensuring the survival of the colony.

on friendly terms with their more sedentary cousins, were driven by hunger to frequent raids, their intensity such that several pueblos had to be abandoned. By the last few decades of the 17th century, the 80 or so Indian villages extant at Onate's arrival had shrunk to fewer than half that number.

It had become too much to bear. In August of 1680, the Pueblos, finally—if loosely—confederated under the leadership of a San Juan medicine man, Po-Pay, charged south from Taos, killing and burning as they came. The new governor of New Mexico, Antonio de Otermin, had been warned about the rebellion, but simply could not give credence to the reports. Profiting from Spanish arrogance, their ranks now swollen by Apache recruits, the Pueblos moved on Santa Fe, cutting off the water supply and laying siege to the city. The Spaniards were forced to withdraw. As their terrified ranks moved south, the Indians just let them go. They had successfully driven the invaders from their lands; this astonishing feat, the Pueblo Revolt of 1680, remains unparalleled in the history of Native American resistance.

The Revolt took the lives of nearly 400 of the 2,900 Spanish inhabitants of New Mexico, including 21 of the 33 priests then at work in the province, the Indians meting out particularly harsh revenge to the desecrators of their kivas. A defeat so shocking put Spain at a distinct disadvantage to France and England, her rivals for territory in the New World; immediate reconquest was imperative. But despite some furious forays, it took the Spanish 12 long years to re-establish their foothold in New Mexico. The man who finally accomplished the difficult task was yet another in the line of wealthy adventurers associated with the province: Don Diego de Vargas, the illustrious scion of a noble family.

Vargas' success was probably due less to his gifts as a strategist than to the irretrievable nature of the changes worked upon the Pueblo Indians. However much they may have longed to recapture the world they had lost with the intrusion of Coronado, the fact was, as historian Marc Simmons has pointed out, "scarcely a Pueblo alive in 1680 could remember how affairs had stood before the Spaniards brought them cattle and sheep, exotic vegetables and grain, iron hardware and a new religion." During the harsh years under the Spanish yoke, the Indians had become, tragically, something quite different from what they once had been.

After an initial, surprisingly peaceful reconnaissance in 1692, Vargas assured the Viceroy of New Spain that recolonization would be an easy task. But the actual reconquest in 1693 was a bloody affair, and it was followed by another three years of savage skirmishes between Pueblos and Spaniards. By 1696, however, most of the Indians had been put down.

There had been some gains. Although the friars moved quickly to re-establish their missions, never again would they act so brutally to quash native religion. Outwardly embracing Christianity, the Pueblos continued to practice their own rites; the Franciscans, sadder but wiser, now looked the other way. Further, unlike other Indians of the West, the Pueblos greatly benefitted from the extensive land grants "given" to them by the Spanish crown. Although it may have been hard to stomach the thought of being granted territory that had belonged to them from time immemorial, these grants helped the Pueblos retain title to their homelands during the 19th century, when other native peoples were losing theirs and going begging.

But in spite of these benefits, in spite of the new mood of peaceful coexistence between Spaniards and Pueblos through the 18th century, the toll taken by conquest was a terrible one. By the end of the century, the Pueblo population was only half what it had been just a hundred years before, and only one fourth what it had been when the Spaniards first arrived. Of the nearly 80 pueblos that had flourished as Spaniards first marched into New Mexico, only 19 remained; of these, only four—Isleta, Acoma, Taos and Picuris—stood on the same spots they had occupied before the conquest.

The Spaniards, it must be said, were not the only people responsible for the tragic decline of the Pueblos. Throughout the 18th century, the entire province of New Mexico was terrorized, its population—Spanish and Pueblo alike—murdered and captured, its crops stolen and burned by roving bands of Indian raiders: Navajo, Apache and a particularly fierce group that had only recently thundered in, newly on horseback, from the northern plains—the Comanche.

In parties sometimes numbering a thousand or more warriors, the raiders would sweep down on tiny Spanish settlements, on outlying haciendas, on undefended pueblos. Horses, cattle and other livestock would be stolen, along with food and other goods; even worse was the wholesale slaughter of men and women, and the kidnapping of children to be sold for ransom or into slavery. Hardly a family was immune from this kind of heartbreaking loss; as Marc Simmons has noted, "The magnitude of the suffering and destruction experienced by colonial New Mexicans [at the hands of raiding tribes] can scarcely be imagined today." The more remote settlements were suddenly either bristling with fortifications (the farming community of Ranchos de Taos, for example, was once surrounded by high walls some six feet thick) or were abandoned; refugees poured into Santa Fe and the newer villas of Santa Cruz and Albuquerque; once again, the future of the colony was threatened.

The man who stepped in to save the day was Juan Bautista de Anza, an honest, vigorous diplomat and wily Indian fighter of long standing. In 1778, Anza arrived in Santa Fe to assume the office of governor, determined to put an end to the Indians' wildly disrupting hit-and-run attacks. Proceeding on the principle of divide and conquer, Anza began with the Comanche, routing the infamous chief Cuerno Verde ("Green Horn," so named for his distinctive headdress decorated with a green-painted buffalo horn) and his band in the late summer of 1779. He then sued for peace, and although it took him several years to achieve it (a treaty was not agreed upon until 1786), when it came, it was a triumph for Anza: one of the longer-lasting arrangements in the history of the West, it enabled Hispanics and Pueblos to move freely among the Comanche even a century later, when Anglos in the same territory were in constant fear for their lives. Moreover, it proved extremely effective in cutting back the activities of other hostiles in New Mexico, for under its terms, the Comanche allied themselves with the Spaniards, joining them in the fight against the Apache.

By the end of the 18th century, then, growth of the New Mexican colony, which had slowed drastically because of the Indian wars, had picked up again. A steady stream of immigrants moved north from New Spain, most settling in tiny communities tucked into the hills and glens abutting the Rio Grande Valley. There they found themselves part of an isolated but extremely varied society, made up of Spaniards, *mestizos* (those of mixed blood), Indians and *genízaros* (Indians not native to New Mexico, but who had been brought there as captives and then ransomed). These groups lived together

A wagon train arrives triumphantly in Santa Fe, the end of the trail, circa 1844.

formal church. Moreover, the group evolved into a political and sociological force, offering care for the sick, help for the poor and counsel for the troubled and bereaved.

Still today, private Penitente *moradas* (chapels) may be seen in the tiny hamlets of the Sangre de Cristos. Many of these villages, in fact, have retained much of their 18th-century character. In the whitewashed adobe churches and cramped adobe houses, an antique Spanish is still spoken; the people with their timeless faces still work the same tiny plots of land handed down by their ancestors, planting the same crops of beans and squash, corn and chili. Truchas, Trampas, Los Ojos: they might just as well be Brigadoon—it seems impossible that the outside world could ever intrude.

But of course, it did, in 1806, in the form of one Zebulon Pike. Sent by the brash new government of the brash new United States, Pike was supposed to be looking for the headwaters of the Arkansas and Red rivers, thought to be part of the recent Louisiana Purchase. He led his party across the plains to the foot of the Colorado Rockies, endured a miserable winter, then crossed the mountains and erected a stockade on a tributary of the Rio Grande, claiming (or at least pretending) to believe that he was on the upper reaches of the Red River, and so still in American territory. He learned the error of his ways when he was arrested and escorted to Santa Fe by a group of mounted soldiers sent out by panicked colonial officials. Repeatedly interrogated, Pike gave little or nothing away; his maps, drawings and notes were confiscated and he and his men were released in Louisiana.

Back at home, Pike wrote, from memory, a book about his experiences, the first description of the huge lands west of the Mississippi to reach the general public. Interest in his account ran high, particularly among those who saw its economic significance. Manufactured goods, Pike reported, were in scant supply throughout the province; when available, they sold for staggeringly high prices. The implications were obvious. Fortunes were waiting to be made by anyone who could tap this vast, untouched market.

Those who tried were, initially, met with hostility. Spanish restrictions on commerce and travel were stringent; unauthorized traders were imprisoned, their goods impounded. To the Spaniards, the Americans posed a very real threat; they were certainly not to be welcomed with open

with a degree of freedom and social mobility unknown in other areas of New Spain, most as independent—if frequently poverty-stricken—subsistence farmers. In their isolation, they developed their own culture, their own ways of living, even their own religious practices, all distinctively New Mexican.

A case in point was the development of Los Hermanos Penitentes, a religious brotherhood commonly known as the Penitentes. Too often left to their own devices by the Mother Church, many Hispanic villagers—particularly those in northern New Mexico's mountain communities—devised their own rites, seeking forgiveness for their sins and for the death of Christ on the Cross. Spiritual pain and its earthly concomitant, physical pain, were important parts of the Penitente proceedings; flagellation and the reenactment of the Crucifixion, with one of the brotherhood standing in for Christ, were practices that brought the group significant notoriety. Banned by the Church several times, forced to operate in secrecy, the brotherhood nevertheless persisted, for it served a real need, satisfying the religious yearnings of those isolated from the arms, however fierce the hunger for their tantalizing wares: bolts of cloth, packets of pins and cards of buttons, hats and gloves, glassware and furniture and gleaming metal tools. It was only with Mexican independence from Spain, in 1821, that the harsh restrictions were lifted, enabling American traders to open full-fledged business with New Mexico. Among these traders was one William Becknell, a Missouri man who, only three months after the bells of freedom rang in Mexico City, entered Santa Fe at the head of a pack train; for his daring and initiative in blazing a path into the Southwest, he has earned the title, "Father of the Santa Fe Trail."

The history of the Santa Fe Trail is the stuff of legend; what seems truly amazing is the speed with which the epic developed. Once the sluice gates were open, traders began to pour over the two branches of the trail into Santa Fe, first in a trickle, then in a flood. Traffic along the trail was eventually so heavy that even today, a century after the last wagon rolled westward, ruts driven deep into the earth by countless wheel-rims still may be seen from Missouri to New Mexico. The sheer volume of trade far exceeded anything that representatives of the Mexican government had been able to imagine; all too quickly, it allowed Anglo-Americans to move into New Mexico, establishing control over its economy.

Meanwhile, Anglo-American and French-Canadian fur trappers were making their way into northern New Mexico in pursuit of beaver pelts, highly prized during this era for toppers worn by the fashionable gents of London, Paris and New York. Operating mostly without licenses and in direct violation of Mexican law, the mountain men earned fortunes and reputations; the most famous of them, Christopher "Kit" Carson (see page 42), would become one of New Mexico's most illustrious citizens. With the businessmen who also profited from the fur trade (most notably the Bent brothers, Charles and William, and the dashing Ceran St. Vrain), the mountain men joined the traders of the Santa Fe Trail both in altering New Mexico's economy and in breaking down the isolation that had separated the territory from the outside world.

Soon New Mexico's ties with the United States began to seem stronger than those that bound it to Mexico. The insensitive appointment of a non-New Mexican governor,

DENNIS & MARIA HENRY

Wagon ruts of the Santa Fe Trail, still visible today near Turkey Creek crossing north of Clayton.

Colonel Albino Perez, in 1835, drove the dividing wedge even further. Perez exacerbated the situation by announcing new taxes and seemingly arbitrary regulations; when, in 1837, he ordered the arrest of a popular alcalde, rebellion broke out. Perez was seized and decapitated, his head ghoulishly sported with by the rebels.

But the final challenge to Mexican rule in New Mexico did not come until 1846, when war broke out between the United States and Mexico. Although some American opposition to the war existed (primarily from anti-slavery elements who feared the expansion of slave-holding territories), Manifest Destiny beckoned, and once Texas had been annexed in 1845, the rich territories of New Mexico and California could not be far behind. The tricky element, however, was finding a way to take these lands without excessive violence; bloodshed, it was argued, might disrupt the already burgeoning trade on the Santa Fe Trail—and wasn't trade what Manifest Destiny was really all about?

General Stephen W. Kearny and the Army of the West worked the miracle, marching into New Mexico over the mountain branch of the Santa Fe Trail, then down through Las Vegas and on into Santa Fe. Along the way, Kearny

Above: Taos trader Charles Bent, the ill-fated first Anglo governor of the New Mexico Territory, was murdered by insurgents in the Taos Rebellion of 1847.

Right top: The trackless plains and endless skies of eastern New Mexico, much the same today as when viewed by travelers on the Santa Fe Trail.
Right: The low adobe town of Santa Fe, set at the foot of the Sangre de Cristo mountains, circa 1846.

delivered speech after reassuring speech: "Not a pepper, not an onion shall be taken by my troops without pay...I will protect you in your persons and property and in your religion." Accepting the inevitable—for the moment—New Mexicans capitulated, quietly accepting American rule. Without firing a shot, Kearny entered and claimed Santa Fe, the job rendered that much easier by the fact that Governor Manuel Armijo already had fled the city, blaming and denouncing as he ran.

New Mexico "conquered," Kearny went to work with a will, appointing Taos trader Charles Bent as its first Anglo governor and working out a legal framework, later known as the Kearny Code, to ensure that the governmental transition would be a smooth one. He then moved on to California, believing that the American occupation of New Mexico was secure.

It was not. Many of the territory's Hispanic residents were no happier at the advent of American rule than the Indians had been with the arrival of the Spanish. In Taos, in 1847, the two old enemies joined forces, Hispanic dissidents and Taos Indians uniting in revolt. Governor Bent, up from Santa Fe for a hometown visit, was slain, his scalp paraded on a board through the Taos streets. American forces struck back quickly. When 700 rebels barricaded themselves in the Pueblo's mission church, refusing to surrender, the American commander shelled the church, literally blowing it to bits. One hundred fifty insurrectionists were killed; seven others were later executed for their part in the plot. The tumbled walls of the bombarded church are still visible at Taos Pueblo, their ruins an evocative enclosure for what is now the pueblo graveyard.

By March of 1848, the Mexican War was over. By the terms of the peace agreement, the Treaty of Guadalupe Hidalgo, Mexico recognized Texas as part of the United States, with the Rio Grande as its southern boundary; further, the United States gained from Mexico all the lands occupied by its forces, including California and New Mexico, the latter at this time encompassing most of the present-day Southwest.

Border disputes would continue for some time, not only with Mexico, but also with Texas, which tried to claim much of eastern New Mexico—all the way, in fact, to Santa Fe. The situation was rendered particularly ticklish by the fact that

Texas was a slave state; New Mexicans had gone on record in 1848 as being opposed to slavery. Texas was appeased by Congress with the Compromise of 1850, which gave the Lone Star state $10 million in exchange for the relinquishment of all claims on eastern New Mexico. There are those who contend that Texas gave up such claims in name only, and has been trying to wrest the territory back, if only economically, ever since. Thus the sobriquet, "Poor New Mexico: so far from heaven, so close to Texas."

The Compromise of 1850 also established New Mexico as a territory, rather than a state, its officials not elected locally but appointed from far-off Washington. This was a great disappointment to many factions, one that was to be repeated over and over again through the remainder of the 19th century. During more than 60 years as an American territory, New Mexico was bypassed for statehood 15 times, largely, it has been suspected, because of racism. New Mexico was too "different," too "foreign," too teeming, some would bluntly proclaim, with "colored" races. Not until 1912 would conditions—and minds—change enough to allow New Mexico admission as the 47th state in the Union.

The American conquest of the New Mexico Territory was followed by a decade of rapid growth and accompanying change. The Gadsden Purchase of 1853 added enormous acreage to southern New Mexico; no sooner had the purchase been made than settlers moved in. The fertile Mesilla Valley, also in the southern portion of the territory, was beginning to rival the valley of the Rio Grande in agricultural production. Intrepid explorers were pushing north into what would become Colorado Territory, and west, into what would be Arizona. In 1858, John Butterfield's Overland Mail company inaugurated twice-weekly stage service between St. Louis and San Francisco, linking New Mexico to both the East and the West. And dotting the entire landscape were new and bustling forts, established to provide protection to traders; travelers and settlers alike.

But the business of building the territory was dramatically interrupted by the advent of the Civil War. However much New Mexicans may have wished to avoid the conflict, their position was too strategic for either side to ignore. The Confederates, dreaming of creating an empire that would stretch to the Pacific, immediately marched into the territory,

DENNIS & MARIA HENRY

moving from Texas up the Rio Grande. But despite some initial success, the Confederates could not win a decisive battle. They were hampered not only by stubborn Union Army resistance, but also by the territory's Hispanic population, whose passionate hatred of the Confederacy's Texan troops had not been anticipated. Soundly trounced in March of 1862 at the decisive Battle of Glorieta Pass (often referred to as the Gettysburg of the West), Confederate forces stumbled south to Texas; New Mexico's participation in the Civil War was, effectively, over.

The effects of the war on the territory, however, were only beginning. First, by 1863, enough attention had been focused on the Southwest to make Congress realize what a huge, ungovernable chunk of land they were dealing with; they decided to split off the western half of the New Mexico Territory, creating the territory of Arizona. New Mexicans accepted this action with equanimity; their smaller territory would be easier to handle, and they were grateful that it still

Seven hundred insurgents barricaded themselves in the San Geronimo mission church at Taos Pueblo during the Taos Rebellion of 1847; after the church was shelled and 150 rebels killed, the ruins were left to enclose the pueblo graveyard.

TWO FRIARS

MUSEUM OF NEW MEXICO

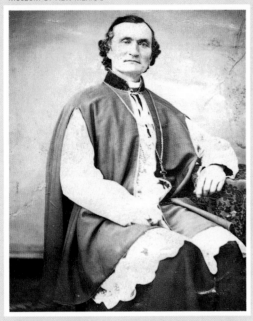

Much of the stern character of Archbishop Jean Baptiste Lamy may be seen in this telling photograph, taken sometime in the 1860s.

Given the fact that New Mexico was settled as much by priests as by soldiers, it is hardly surprising that churchmen had a continuing influence on the territory for several hundred years. But perhaps none was as influential as Jean Baptiste Lamy, the man who for much of the 19th century led New Mexico's Catholic Church, first as bishop, then, after 1875, as archbishop.

The model for the saintly Latour in Willa Cather's *Death Comes for the Archbishop*, the real-life Lamy was a prickly combination of the genuinely devout and the decidedly ambitious. A Frenchman by birth, Lamy spoke little Spanish when he arrived in Santa Fe in 1851. Despite this handicap, he immediately grasped the seriousness of the situation confronting him: the native clergy's way of living was not only undisciplined, he believed—it was a scandal. The long years of isolation had allowed license to flourish. Father Jose Manuel Gallegos of Albuquerque, for example, supplemented his priestly duties by operating a store...which he kept open on Sundays...under the supervision of his mistress.

Such iniquities had to be stopped. Lamy clamped down, instituting a program of tough but necessary reforms. During his tenure, he also built 45 new churches—including the cathedral at Santa Fe—and a string of parochial schools that provided the only education some New Mexicans ever would receive. While these were major accomplishments, Lamy often found himself at odds with local clergy and parishioners, who insisted that he had little understanding of New Mexico's special needs and customs, and who feared that Lamy's actions would severely alter the particular character of the area's Hispanic Catholicism. Chief among Lamy's opponents was Father Antonio Jose Martinez of Taos.

A native New Mexican, born in Abiquiu and raised in Taos, Martinez came late and emotionally to the church, after his wife died in childbirth. He was an intellectual, a patriot and a radical, zealously determined to aid the devout Catholics of his native land, long—he felt—disenfranchised and ignored by the church they revered. Fiery and charismatic, Martinez used his own money to finance a desperately needed school, urged students to become priests in their own homeland, encouraged the government to devote real money and energy to the "civilizing" of warring Indian tribes, and was directly responsible for the 1833 outlawing of formal tithing, a practice that had imposed a harsh financial burden on people simply unable to bear it. Moreover, he tacitly went along with certain religious practices—those of the Penitentes, for example—condemned by other church officials.

Lamy despised virtually everything Martinez stood for. He moved quickly, reinstituting tithing, banning the Penitentes, even attempting to discourage the use of *santos* and *Cristos*, the beautiful—if often disturbing—religious folk carvings that were sometimes the focal point of humble mountain churches and homes. Martinez, of course, fought back. As offended by the Taos friar's political activity as by his unorthodox methods, Lamy excommunicated Martinez in 1857.

Interestingly, although Lamy is the dominant figure of the history books, it is Martinez who still is honored in the tiny communities of northern New Mexico that he defended more than a hundred years ago. There, the Penitentes still practice their rituals, the santos still are carved and old-fashioned Hispanic Catholicism remains the faith of many.

included the important Mesilla Valley, which another proposed plan would have excluded.

An even more critical effect of the Civil War in New Mexico was the consequent renewal here of Indian fighting. Apache and Navajo swiftly noted the white men at each other's throats, abandoning forts and withdrawing troops for duty in the East; believing that they would face little or no opposition, they stepped up raids on civilian settlements. The nightmare quality of these raids was soon matched, then exceeded, horror for horror, by the American response.

General James Carleton and his California Column arrived to take charge of the military Department of New Mexico in the fall of 1862; immediately, Carleton turned his considerable energies to the "Indian problem," reopening existing forts, building new ones and announcing a formal policy. He would warn all Indian leaders that failure to keep the peace would result in swift punishment; he would send troops to pacify Indians who continued to raid, with the intention of defeating, not negotiating with, them; once they had been defeated, the Indians would be brought to permanent reservations, where they would become Christian farmers, their lives to be directed henceforth by the government.

Carleton did, in fact, carry out each point of his plan; the result was failure of the most dismal kind. Warned, the Navajo and Apache nevertheless continued to raid. So, utilizing the Indian-fighting experience of a surprisingly reluctant Kit Carson, Carleton harried first the Mescalero Apach, then the Navajo into submission, interning them at the Bosque Redondo Reservation, 1,600 square miles of lonely grassland by the bitter waters of the Pecos River.

The story of the campaign against the Navajos, in particular, might be written in tears. Hunted down like dogs, driven into the most remote canyons of their domain where resistance meant starvation, they were, further, spared no humiliation. Not content to kill and capture, American forces pointlessly laid Navajo land waste, even, on several occasions, chopping down groves of peach trees that had been lovingly tended for generations. Finally convinced that their choices were capitulation or extermination, the Navajo agreed to go to the Bosque Redondo. There followed one of the most shameful episodes in the often shameful history of American-Indian relations: the Long Walk, a forced march from the

MUSEUM OF NEW MEXICO

Captive Indians labor at Fort Sumner during the Bosque Redondo internment, circa 1864 to 1866.

Navajo homeland in northwestern New Mexico to the new reservation watched over by Fort Sumner in the southeast. Along the way, many Indians sickened and died, others were captured by marauding bands of Utes and Hispanics, hoping for ransom money.

At Bosque Redondo, things went from bad to worse. The Navajo and Mescalero Apache did not get along; the poor soil and worse water could not support their numbers; disease spread; Indians starved while their soldier guardians ate beefsteak. By 1865, the Mescalero simply abandoned the reservation, returning to their homelands in the Sacramento Mountains. In 1873, the U.S. government, belatedly realizing that its efforts to relocate them had failed, officially established a permanent reservation for the Mescalero in the Sacramentos.

The Navajo remained at the Bosque Redondo, in deplorable conditions, until 1868. That year, they were given three options: if they promised never again to fight, they could remain at the Bosque Redondo, move to a reservation with

Above: Geronimo, the brilliant and redoubtable strategist of the Chiricahua Apache, 1884.
Right: A wagon train of the 1870s in the plaza at Santa Fe. In background of photograph: Archbishop Lamy's unfinished cathedral.

Facing page, top: Work train, crew and canine mascot at Engle in 1890.
Bottom: Abetted by the railroad boom, New Mexico's lumber industry flourished in the last decades of the 19th century. Here, W.W. McAlpine's bustling sawmill, near Catskill.

good soil and water to be set aside for them in what was then Indian Territory, or they could return to the harsh, sere territory of northwestern New Mexico and northeastern Arizona, their former homeland. To the Americans' surprise, the Navajo unanimously chose the third option, passionately proclaiming, "[We] hope to God you will not ask us to go to any country but our own...Our God created it specifically for us." The land finally meted out for their reservation was a much smaller area than that which the Navajo once had roamed; nevertheless, they retreated to it with dignity and some small measure of content. Never again would they ride forth to raid.

Following the example of the Mescalero and the Navajo, the Jicarilla Apache soon agreed to move to a permanent reservation in northern New Mexico. So it was left to the Chiricahua Apache to write the final chapter in the history of the New Mexican Indian Wars. With a series of brilliant strategists—Victorio, Nana and Geronimo—as their leaders, the Chiricahua held out in the deserts and canyons of southwestern New Mexico and southeastern Arizona until 1886. Finally forced to surrender, all 502 remaining Chiricahua were sent to prison in Florida, then relocated to Oklahoma. In 1913, 187 Chiricahua were granted the right to return in peace to New Mexico, where they settled quietly on the reservation with their cousins, the Mescalero. At the very least, they were home at last.

Pueblo Indians, meanwhile, existed in a state of shocking neglect for most of the latter half of the 19th century. Where Mexico had recognized them as citizens and had made special provisions for the protection of their property rights, the United States was unwilling to extend similar treatment, not even deigning to distinguish them, on many occasions, from warring nomadic tribes. Over and over again, the Pueblos petitioned for assistance, asking for voting rights, educational opportunities and aid in defending their valuable irrigated lands from the countless squatters who continually harassed them. Little was done. After 1854, the United States Surveyor General did confirm the Pueblo land grants, but the government's responsibility to provide active protection from encroachment was not recognized until 1913.

During this era, only one gesture was made toward the Pueblos, honorary and empty. In 1863, Abraham Lincoln, grateful that they had remained neutral during the Western Civil War, sent each Pueblo governor a silver-headed cane, engraved with the date and his name. However hollow the gesture, the canes were treasured, and to this day play a part in Pueblo ceremonials.

With the Civil War over, and the Indian threat soon diminished or eliminated, New Mexico began, at last, to open up to the world. As it did, the face of the land changed forever. Sheepmen fanned out first, trailing their flocks as far east as the Llano Estacado, as far west as the San Juan Basin. Before long, they were joined—and in many cases overrun—by the great herds of the cattlemen. As early as 1866, Charles Goodnight and Oliver Loving—two of the most romantically named men in a very romantic history—drove stock up from Texas over what would soon be known as the Goodnight-

Loving Trail, one of the great cattle thoroughfares of the West. They were soon joined by others who knew a good thing when they saw it. New Mexico's most famous stockman became John S. Chisum, whose holdings ran for 150 miles along the Pecos River, and whose more devious dealings contributed to the infamous Lincoln County War.

Originally planning to market their beef at the Bosque Redondo and other Indian reservations, the cattlemen saw whole new markets opening up with the rapid development of mining districts throughout the territory, and particularly in the rugged mountains of the southeast. The ancient dreams of the Spaniards were suddenly coming true, with strike after strike of gold and silver: Pinos Altos in 1860, Elizabethtown in 1866, Silver City in 1869, Hillsboro in 1877, White Oaks in 1879, Kingston in 1883, Lake Valley in 1887, and Mogollon in 1889.

Almost simultaneously, the railroad finally arrived in New Mexico, the result of a period of frantic building during which workers sometimes laid as much as a mile and a half of track in a single day. The Atchison, Topeka & Santa Fe Railroad entered New Mexico in 1879, plunging over the Raton Pass and south through Las Vegas and Albuquerque. By 1880, another line, the Southern Pacific Railroad, had arrived from the west; in 1881, the two met at Deming. Now New Mexico had a transcontinental railroad route—only the second of its kind—which meant that its inhabitants could travel and ship goods to both East and West coasts.

It also meant that newcomers at last had easy access to the territory; soon, they were arriving in droves. New Mexico's expanding economy could provide employment opportunities in the mines, in the relatively new lumber industry (another offshoot of the railroad boom), in ranching and— for those willing to struggle—in farming. Most who came to farm meant to take advantage of the Homestead Act, which offered 160-acre plots of public land to whoever would work and "prove up" the land within a set period of time, usually five years. Homesteads in the eastern part of the territory were quickly snapped up; almost as quickly, many homesteaders lost their farms to the ravages of drought. Those who remained did so only because they were able to adjust to the exigencies of the climate, becoming experts (like the Spaniards and Indians before them) at dry farming.

With the influx of farmers and miners, railroad men and ranchers, there also came a flood of investors, speculators and lawyers, eager to profit from quickly rising real estate values. Old land grant titles constituted a thorny legal thicket; fraud proliferated. In 1891, Congress set up the Court of Private Land Claims; by 1903, this court had ruled on all land grant claims. Not surprisingly, when the dust had cleared, some 80 percent of Spanish and Mexican land grants ended up in the hands of Anglo lawyers and recent settlers. One land grant lawyer alone, Thomas B. Catron, wound up with outright ownership of 2 million acres, and a share in an additional 4 million.

Even more land—and particularly the *ejidos*, territory once held communally by Hispanic villagers, where they farmed, grazed sheep, cut wood, hunted and fished—was swept up by the Bureau of Land Management and the United States Forest Service. If they wanted to continue to use this land for hunting or grazing, Hispanics now had to compete for the right with large-scale Anglo ranchers. They were required to apply and pay for permits and licenses—this, for the use of land that had been theirs for 200 years or more. Suddenly, many Hispanics found themselves suffering from the same ills to which they had formerly subjected the Indians.

These iniquities seemed particularly painful because, up until the 1940s, Hispanics were New Mexico's largest demographic group and, in many ways, the culturally dominant one. Both Hispanic and Indian influences, certainly, were what gave—and continue to give—the state its special character, a mix of the exotic, the colorful and the spiritual that soon was drawing a new kind of immigrant: artists, writers and other intellectuals. Attracted by a seductively different way of life and held by a landscape stranger and more beautiful than any they had previously known were such diverse characters as patron of the arts Mabel Dodge Luhan, internationally renowned writers D.H. Lawrence, Oliver LaFarge and John Collier, and painters Bert Phillips, Ernest Blumenschein, Andrew Dasburg and, later, John Marin, John Sloan, Marsden Hartley and Georgia O'Keeffe, the artist who, perhaps more than any other, has come to be associated with New Mexico (see overleaf: New Mexico and the Arts).

Some believe that the art colony denizens occasionally exploited native peoples, perpetuating certain stereotypes for the benefit of the tourist trade. But the Pueblo Indians, in particular, could not have had better friends in their battle against the Bursum Bill, a critical piece of national legislation introduced in 1922. Instigated by Albert B. Fall, the New Mexican politician who had just been named Secretary of the Interior by President Warren G. Harding, the bill was designed to give non-Indians title to all Pueblo land they had gained before 1902—in many cases, by illegal means. Further, the bill would have permitted state courts—notoriously unfriendly to Native Americans—to settle all future disputes over land titles. By extension, it also would have given state judges the authority to force native priests, governors and other officials to reveal information about the most secret aspects of Pueblo religious life, or face contempt citations. In short, the Bursum Bill spelled disaster for the Pueblos, particularly since they were kept uninformed about it by the Bureau of Indian Affairs, which evidently hoped it could be passed in secrecy.

Enter the young poet, John Collier, who, learning of the bill, rallied other members of the Taos and Santa Fe art colonies to the Indians' cause. While the Indians themselves, now alerted to the danger facing them, formed an All-Pueblo Council (their first gesture of unification since the Pueblo Revolt of 1680) and sent a delegation in protest to Washington, the artists and writers busied themselves with a stream of protests, rallies, letters and resolutions. The campaign worked: public outrage was roused nationwide, the Bursum Bill was withdrawn, and in 1924 the Pueblo Lands Act confirmed, for good and all, the ancient land rights extended to the Pueblos by Spain. Implicated in the Teapot Dome Scandal, Albert Fall became the first cabinet member in U.S. history to be sent to prison for crimes committed while in office; in 1933, John Collier was appointed Commissioner for Indian Affairs by President Franklin D. Roosevelt.

The attention focused on New Mexico by the fight over the Bursum Bill led to new interest in the state's landscape and its cultural heritage. Encouraged, first Indians, then Hispanics experienced a renaissance in their arts and crafts, music and folk drama. These attractions, along with newly developed state and national parks and monuments, gave rise to a burgeoning tourist industry, which helped to sustain the state during the darker days of the Great Depression.

But not much could be done to aid New Mexican farmers, particularly the dry farmers of the East Side. Economically devastated, they were also plagued by a prolonged drought that turned their lands to dust, and by winds that whipped the dust into frightening "black rollers," huge clouds sometimes measuring hundreds of feet high and miles across. In all parts of New Mexico, farm land plunged in worth, bottoming out at $4.95 an acre, the lowest value per acre in the United States.

Ironically, it was the Second World War that finally brought the state out of the Depression, with the inauguration of a whole new industry that had its wellspring in a secret village built high on the Pajarito Plateau in northern New Mexico: Los Alamos (see page 45). There a group of scientists, working at times within a few hundred yards of the Anasazi ruins of Tyuonyi, propelled New Mexico—and the world—

(continued on page 41)

Above: "Cowboys Going to Dinner"— and looking mighty happy about it, too. Mora County, 1897.

Facing page, top: Corn continued to be a staple for Hispanic farmers, as it had been for their Pueblo predecessors. Here a family husks a bumper crop, circa 1905.
***Bottom:** Farmers threshing with sheep and goats near Santa Fe, circa 1915.*

NEW MEXICO & THE ARTS

One of the pre-eminent painters of our age, Georgia O'Keeffe, relaxing in the New Mexico that gave her the subject matter for her greatest work.

It seems inevitable, somehow—New Mexico's status as virtual border-to-border art colony. All the natural drawing cards are there: the invigorating climate, the incandescent light, the stunning sweep of gilded desert, red rock, turquoise sky. Then there is the magical cultural hodge-podge: the combination of Indian, Hispanic and Anglo influences is a powerful stimulant to creativity, as is the checkered history of the three cultures' centuries of crisis and clash. Finally, there is the simple fact that creative work of the most exemplary kind has been done in New Mexico from prehistoric times. The finely hewn stonework of an Anasazi kiva, the inquisitive owl staring forth from a Mimbres olla, the bold reds and blacks of a Navajo chief's blanket, the exquisitely carved and colored face of a Hispanic santo, the drama of the San Ildefonso deer dance: all these and more form the natural base on which so much of the more formalized art of the last hundred years has been built.

The first of the state's self-conscious art colonies—and the most enduring—came together as the result of a happy accident. In the 1890s, artist Joseph Henry Sharp meandered through Taos on a sketching trip, bringing back tales of the area's high clear light and exotic ambiance to fellow Eastern artists Ernest Blumenschein and Bert Phillips. Blumenschein and Phillips remembered the stories when, on their own painting expedition some time later, a wheel of their wagon broke some 30 miles from Taos. Blumenschein took it to town for repairs and never left; Phillips soon joined him; and in 1915, with Sharp and others, they formed the Taos Society of Artists, the seed of one of America's most influential art-based communities.

Nineteen-sixteen saw the arrival of Mabel Dodge, a New York heiress and patron of the arts then married to painter Maurice Sterne. Utterly captured by Taos, she made it her home, building a large and beautiful adobe house and marrying Taos Indian Antonio Luhan, her fourth (and final) husband. A flurry of telegrams and train tickets went out; most of Mrs. Luhan's New York salon soon followed. Typical was painter Andrew Dasburg, who received his ticket with a cable which read, "Wonderful place. You must come." He obeyed, staying for the rest of his life.

Even the illustrious D.H. Lawrence was lured to New Mexico by Mrs. Luhan; he was grateful. "I think," he would write, "New Mexico was the

greatest experience from the outside world that I have ever had. It certainly changed me forever." Mrs. Luhan, also, was changed; her marriage to Tony Luhan turned out to be a good one, and she wrote, from her lovely house in Taos, some remarkable books reflecting a deep if eccentric spirituality and a genuine love for her adopted town.

By the 1920s, other parts of the state were also becoming major centers for the arts. Albuquerque was home to brother and sister writers Harvey Fergusson and Erna Fergusson, whose family had entered the state over the Santa Fe Trail. Established writer Mary Austin arrived in Santa Fe in 1918; her "Land of Journey's Ending" found indigenous Pueblo culture superior to any other culture found elsewhere in the United States. Austin attracted other writers to Santa Fe, including Willa Cather (whose *Death Comes for the Archbishop* was conceived and largely written while she was visiting Austin), Witter Bynner and Oliver LaFarge (who won the Pulitzer Prize in 1929 for his novel about Indian life, *Laughing Boy*).

Santa Fe soon had a colony of artists to rival that of Taos. John Sloan, Marsden Hartley, Arthur Dove and John Marin all did major work from the capital city. And by the end of the 1920s, a first visit had been made, not to Taos or Santa Fe, but to remote and wildly beautiful Abiquiu by the artist who would make the most famous New Mexican paintings of them all:

Georgia O'Keeffe. By the time she died, almost 100 years old, O'Keeffe had been recognized as one of America's greatest modern painters, and had created landscapes of stark beauty and unrivalled power.

The Anglo art colonies soon repaid their debt of inspiration to native artisans. A new appreciation for both Indian and Hispanic arts led to revivals in the making of Pueblo pottery (the stunning black-on-black ware of San Ildefonso potter Maria Martinez was a product of this period), Navajo blankets and rugs, Chimayo blankets, Navajo and Pueblo silverwork, and Hispanic woodcarving and *colcha* (embroidery); these revivals continue apace today, encouraged by the many festivals and craft fairs held throughout the state, and with the example always of the beautiful items on display in such outstanding collections as those of the Museum of International Folk Art, the Museum of Fine Arts and the Wheelwright Museum of the American Indian in Santa Fe; Albuquerque's Indian Pueblo Cultural Center; and the Millicent Rogers Museum in Taos.

Appreciation for the performing arts, too, seems to have its roots in enthusiasm for native spectacles, particularly the complex religious ceremonials of the Apache, Navajo and Pueblo peoples. A combination of dance, music and high drama, these rites may be viewed today in much the same form in which they have existed for a millenium; they are a vivid glimpse of

New Mexico's—and mankind's—past. Rites with more modern antecedants are on view at the countless musical and theatrical events crowding the calendar statewide, perhaps most notably at the Santa Fe Opera. Now in its fourth decade of operation, this company has earned an international reputation, not least because of the opera house's dramatic open-air perch overlooking the valley of the Rio Grande.

Writers such as Paul Horgan, Frank Waters, Rudolfo Anaya, Leslie Marmon Silko, Tony Hillerman and John Nichols, and such artists as Peter Hurd, R.C. Gorman, Ken Price and George Lopez are current contributors to New Mexico's ongoing love affair with the arts. As long as the skies stay blue and the air remains wine-like, as long as cultural turmoil keeps the sociological atmosphere at a nice, rolling boil, it seems likely that the affair will continue, as passionate and involving as it has ever been.

MUSEUM OF NEW MEXICO PHOTOS BOTH PAGES

Top: Taos artist W. Herbert Dunton not only painted Western art, he dressed for the occasion.
Above: Taos artist Walter Ufer at work, 1927.

126
6-6-1915

ELICK BEAM OLD SPANISH MINE

into the nuclear age. The first atomic bomb was tested on July 16, 1945 at Trinity Site in the desolate White Sands, just at the southern edge—appropriately—of the Jornada del Muerto.

In the post-war period, New Mexico has remained in the forefront of atomic research, with the Los Alamos Scientific Laboratory and the Sandia National Laboratories leading the way. Weapons and missile testing take place at the Sandia Military Base near Albuquerque and at the White Sands Missile Range, near Alamogordo. The manufacturing of ordnance, electronics and precision instruments—an off-shoot of weapons and defense research—also found a place in the state, bringing in both new money and new people.

Oil and natural gas, uranium, coal and potash have boosted the state's economy, but all these industries experienced a decline during the 1980s. At the same time, many small farms have been consolidated into agribusiness conglomerates. This, together with a centuries-old tradition of dividing land by inheritance (a tradition that occasionally has reached the extreme of apportioning houses room by room, even beam by beam), has left inhabitants of the old Hispanic farming villages with very little from which to eke out a living. The resulting drift of the population to urban centers has altered—perhaps permanently—the traditionally rural character of the state.

Unfortunately, it might be said that the economy of modern New Mexico is very much like that of a Third World country: relying heavily on the export of raw materials and depending on federal spending for programs of no certain permanence, it is largely at the mercy of forces over which it has no control.

One bright spot has been the continued, even accelerated development of the tourist trade. Ever dependable are the state's breathtaking landscape, multifarious recreational opportunities and unique cultural ambiance. Many visitors to the state have been caught by these charms and have decided to stay; despite an uncertain economy, New Mexico—like its Sunbelt neighbors—has seen a surge in population over the last two decades.

Yet this rapid growth in itself has presented new problems, not unrelated to those that have troubled the state in the past. Perhaps the greatest of these has been the cultural clash between the area's once dominant Hispanic residents and the

new wave of Anglo settlers. While Hispanics were a majority of the state's population before 1940, today the majority is Anglo; a sad concomitant of this fact is that, while Hispanics have theoretical equality before the law, in reality, they have become second-class citizens in their own now Anglo-dominated homeland. The Hispanic annual income averages little more than half that of the Anglo, their educational level is lower, they are under-represented in the professions and the percentage of Hispanics living in substandard housing is not only above that of Anglos, but also above that of the few blacks living in the state. Moreover, the steady exodus from farming villages to urban centers has created problems of social and economic adjustment that may take years to resolve.

Hispanic frustration has found outlets in various forms of social protest, the most celebrated being the formation in the early 1960s of the Alianza Federal de Mercedes (Federal Alliance of Land Grants), usually referred to as the Alianza. Led by the charismatic Reies Lopez Tijerina, the Alianza claimed, with some justification, that the loss of the Hispanics' communal lands, the ejidos, led to a corresponding loss

(continued on page 44)

Above: A flock of sheep trailing past Navajo summer and winter hogans, 1940.

Facing page, left: Miner at work in the Santa Rita copper mine, 1915. Unlike the many played-out mines that pock the New Mexican landscape, the Santa Rita still is operating.
Right: A study in contrast: oil rig within sight of the legendary Shiprock, Navajo country, northwestern New Mexico.

41

KIT CARSON

KENT & DONNA DANNEN

Investigate a little, and most folk heroes of the old West turn out to be shadowy figments, more style than substance, mere products of the dime novelist's imagination. Christopher "Kit" Carson, on the other hand, bears scrutiny. A complex character, a real-life hero with a real man's strengths and failings, Carson, like New Mexico, is a mass of contradictions: an illiterate who became a member of high-caste Hispanic society, a lonely mountain man who found himself at home with the most important figures of his day,

an Indian fighter who became an Indian agent and a true friend to the Native Americans with whom he came in contact.

Born in Kentucky in 1809, by the time he was 15, Carson found himself in Old Franklin, Missouri, reluctantly apprenticed to a saddlemaker. When a wagon train bound for Santa Fe passed through town, Carson took the opportunity to run off with it, arriving in New Mexico in 1826. He took up fur trapping, pursuing this career throughout the West for some 15 years, gain-

ing an easy familiarity with the region's vast, beautifully untouched reaches; forming lasting bonds with its original residents, the Indians; and getting to know the grandee society of Taos, then an important capital of the fur trade.

In 1842, a chance encounter with explorer John C. Frémont changed Carson's life, throwing him into the thick of America's greatest push for territory, carried out under the gaudy banner of Manifest Destiny. Carson served as Frémont's principal guide for the government-sponsored explorations of the Far West in 1842 and 1843-1844, and was with him at the conclusion of the third expedition in 1846 when Frémont (probably also with government backing) provoked the infamous Bear Flag Revolt.

By the end of this period, Carson had tired of Frémont's fireworks; he himself was not a man who lived for the limelight. In 1843, he had married Josefa Jaramillo, the daughter of a prominent Taos family; he had secured his position in New Mexican high society; and he had plans to take up a farmstead near his wife's relations. But while en route to Washington, D.C. carrying dispatches for Frémont, he had another chance encounter, this time with General Stephen W. Kearny, just setting out to claim New Mexico and California for the United States. The Mexican War had begun. Kearny pressed, Carson relented; until the war ended in 1848, Carson was kept running with a

combination of fighting, guiding and more dispatch-carrying to Washington, where he earned a well-deserved reputation for bravery, loyalty and unswerving devotion to duty.

After the war, this reputation, joined with a genuine sympathy for the Native American, led to Carson's appointment as Indian Agent at Taos. In spite of the fact that he had been a fierce and, at times, grimly effective Indian fighter, his charges liked and trusted him; he did not, they felt, treat them with condescension. By this time, he was internationally famous; he had been the subject of a melodramatic "biography" by DeWitt Peters, and his fair-haired, blue-eyed countenance was a familiar sight in the rotogravures. But he never learned to read or write much more than his own name, and preferred the relatively quiet life in Taos to the clash and glitter of the world capitals where he would have been welcomed.

Carson's peaceful life was interrupted, however, by the Civil War. He resigned as Agent and accepted a commission as lieutenant colonel under his old fur-trade boss, Ceran St. Vrain, in the First Regiment of New Mexico Volunteers. When St. Vrain left the regiment, Carson became colonel; his largely Hispanic troops respected him, and distinguished themselves in battle.

By 1862, the Confederates had been driven out of the West. But Carson was ill: in 1860, a horse had fallen on him, producing an aortal aneurysm that had gone neglected. Fifty-three years old, aware that further campaigning would be a genuine hardship, wanting to return to his family in Taos, Carson asked for his release from service. It was denied. General James Carleton had taken over as military head of the Department of New Mexico; determined to end the region's "Indian problem" once and for all, he needed Carson—a man who knew the country and the Indians—to implement his plans.

Until recently, Carson was often vilified along with Carleton and other architects of the policy that offered only two choices to the Indians of New Mexico: unconditional surrender or extermination. But lately it has become clear that, far from agreeing with such policy, Carson resisted it. Several times, he asked for his release, suggested that he be assigned to other duty, tried to offer alternatives to the official, brutal line. But Carleton— with Carson as with the Indians—was doggedly persistent; there came a time when Carson's devotion to duty would not allow him to turn down the job again. He rode off first against the Mescalero Apache, then (after another thwarted attempt at resignation) against the Navajo, each time hoping that, at the very least, he might provide a moderating influence.

There is ample evidence that the Indians continued, despite his official position as their conquerer, to regard Carson as their friend. When the Mescalero were beaten near Alamo-gordo by one of Carleton's sub-officers, they nevertheless refused to surrender. Instead, wounded, shaken, they staggered across the mountains to Fort Stanton, where Carson was billeted, preferring to give themselves up to him, a man who might understand them. "We have no more heart," their chief, Cadette, confided to Carson. "Do with us as may seem good to you, but do not forget we are braves and men."

Carson never forgot. Finally released from his onerous duty under Carleton, he returned to his beloved Taos to take charge of Indian Affairs for the newly established Colorado Territory. In 1868, traveling north on Indian business, he was taken ill. He turned back, but before he could reach Taos, he died, felled at last by the long-neglected aneurysm.

Although he is remembered today primarily in the colorful terms of his dime-novel persona, Carson's life is instructive particularly for those who believe that United States policy towards the Indians during the 19th century might somehow be excused on the grounds of ignorance. Men like Carson, who knew the Indians better than most, saw that American policy was wrong; they spoke out against it and tried to change it. That they did not succeed—even when they were men of some influence, as Carson was—offers grim proof of how entrenched that policy was, and how blind to reason.

MUSEUM OF NEW MEXICO

Above: Kit Carson in 1864, during his onerous duty as Indian fighter under General James Carleton; the strain seems to show in his weathered face.
Facing page: The Taos adobe where Carson made his home for a quarter of a century is now a museum.

Homesteading family on the plains near Clovis, circa 1905.

with the modern world. So, although many still earn their livings by traditional methods—farming and raising livestock—the tribes also have diversified their economies in some interesting new ways. The Mescalero Apache, for example, own and operate a ski area, a resort hotel and tourist campgrounds, all in or around their reservation lands in the Sacramento Mountains. The Jicarilla Apache, in northwestern New Mexico, also have developed tourist sites, including a lodge and campgrounds, while the Navajo have successfully managed the rich reserves of coal, oil and uranium found on their lands.

Against such successes must be measured the Native Americans' continuing, severe battle with alcoholism (Gallup, the town in the northwestern part of the state that advertises itself as "the Indian capital of the world" is also known locally as "Drunk City"), and the recurring problems caused by the repeated clash of cultures. Only recently, a Navajo tribal governor was accused of taking kickbacks from Anglo businessmen who used Indians as fronts for their own wheeling-and-dealing schemes. Sadly, his supporters came to his defense by insisting that in an Anglo-dominated society, Indians could succeed as entrepreneurs only if they had Anglo backing, secret or otherwise.

It seems certain that New Mexico's three cultures—Indian, Hispanic, Anglo—will have to learn to forge ahead together to bring the state successfully into the next century. The problems of growth—particularly in terms of overdevelopment and the subsequent threat to the environment—will require the cooperation of all New Mexicans. This is not to imply, however, that any one group must give up its cultural identity in the process; that would be the most tragic loss of all. New Mexico's greatest asset and greatest strength continues to be the existence—side by side but unblended—of excitingly different influences. In this way, the state is very like the nation—and the future of one may well foreshadow the future of the other.

of community and eventually would result in cultural extinction. The group demanded, therefore, the return of the ejidos, and proceeded to back up their demands first with peaceful protest, but ultimately with violence. After its wild 1967 raid on the courthouse at Tierra Amarilla (the main pueblo of an old land grant) led to the shooting of two law officers, the Alianza lost considerable support, but not before providing a voice for many of New Mexico's dispossessed.

The state's Native Americans, meanwhile—Pueblo, Navajo, Apache—were granted citizenship in 1924, although they did not win the right to vote until 1947, and then only by federal mandate. Like their Hispanic neighbors, Native Americans have been plagued by discrimination and its widespread effects: high drop-out rates, massive unemployment, social and psychological displacement. Perhaps because of the many obstacles placed before them, New Mexico's Indians have had to be unusually adaptable in their dealings

LOS ALAMOS AND THE ATOMIC ERA

It was pure chance that made New Mexico the birthplace of the Atomic Age. Searching for a spot where atomic research could be conducted in utmost secrecy, Army Corps of Engineers officials—assigned to construct the facility—consulted with theoretical physicist J. Robert Oppenheimer of the University of California. A native New Yorker, Oppenheimer had spent several idyllic childhood summers on a ranch in the remote Sangre de Cristo Mountains of northern New Mexico. Dimly, he remembered pack trips made to the even more isolated Pajarito Plateau, at the base of the Jemez Mountains. There, Oppenheimer seemed to recall, was a boys' school, a lonely outpost in the wilderness. Perhaps it might, in a pinch, serve.

The Army investigated and agreed. Thirty-five miles from the sleepy town of Santa Fe, its nearest neighbors the San Ildefonso and Santa Clara Pueblos, hard to find and hard to get to, the elite Los Alamos Ranch School was a 7,200-foot-high aerie, perfect for the purpose. By 1942, the school had been appropriated by the government; the following year, a rapidly burgeoning secret city was in place, its population of scientists, military personnel and their bewildered families plunged into the critical race to develop the

Bomb. The Manhattan Project (also referred to as Project Y), headed up by Dr. Oppenheimer, brought together an unprecedented international collection of the most brilliant scientific minds of the day. Niels Bohr, Enrico Fermi, A.H. Compton, I.I. Rabi, Sir James Chadwick, E.O. Lawrence, James B. Conant, among others, participated in the development of "the Gadget," working long hours in difficult conditions to achieve the goal.

Also working hard, in an unparalleled situation, were the unsung wives of the celebrated scientists. Thrust into a strange, often unfriendly environment; forced to live in jerry-built quarters equipped with only the most basic accoutrements (and sometimes not even those: bathtubs, for example, were luxury items on "The Hill"); having to make do despite shortages of food, clothing, fuel and other goods; unable to communicate with their extended families except via censored mail for the duration of the war; and forbidden to know the true nature of their husbands' work, these women persevered cheerfully, catering to discouraged and exhausted spouses, caring for children, creating a lot from a little and, in sum, making The Hill a home.

By July of 1945, miraculously, all the hard work had borne fruit; the Gadget was ready for testing. The Trinity test site was selected in the bleakest part of the Tularosa Basin; later, it would give some scientists pause to realize that this site was at the tail end of the badlands of the Jornada del Muerto, the Journey of Death.

In the moments before dawn on July 16, 1945, the bomb was attached to a steel tower; the last seconds ticked by. Nobody was really sure that the device would work (Oppenheimer himself had bet $10 that it would not), or, if it did, that they would not all be blown to pieces, and the planet along with them. In suspense, everyone waited. Then, at 5:29:45 a.m. Mountain War Time, it came: an incredible burst of light that bathed the mountains in an unearthly glare. A punishing shock wave, an awesome roar of sound, then the steel tower vaporized as a surging multi-colored cloud mushroomed seven miles into the air.

The flash of light was seen in Santa Fe, Silver City, Gallup and El Paso; near Albuquerque, a blind girl riding in a car looked up at the moment of detonation and asked, "What was that?" Two hundred miles away at Los Alamos, one scientist's wife, watching faithfully from The Hill, saw the explosion as a "blinding light like no other light one had ever seen. The trees, illuminated, leaping out. The mountains flashing into life. Later, the long slow rumble. Something had happened, all right, for good or ill."

MUSEUM OF NEW MEXICO

Scientists at Trinity Site, where the first atomic bomb was detonated in July 1945.

Oppenheimer knew right away which it was. He murmured an ancient Hindu quotation: "I am become Death, the destroyer of worlds." He did not fail to see the irony in the fact that he had brought the greatest instrument of destruction the world had ever known to the place he loved best on earth. Nor was he unaware of a further paradox: that one of the most ancient inhabited regions of the United States—and one of the most significantly spiritual in character—had become the birthplace of the most modern—and soulless—of technologies. Chance may have brought New Mexico and the Atomic Age together, but it was a juxtaposition almost too ripe with meaning to be considered arbitrary.

NORTHWEST

PLATEAU COUNTRY AND INDIAN STYLE

CHAPTER THREE

TOM TILL

Above: A gorgeous parade of finely hewn Anasazi doorways, Aztecs Ruins National Monument.

Facing page: Sacred to the Navajo, the stunning Shiprock is an eroded volcanic neck.

This is the classic face of the Old West, immortalized in countless horse operas: deeply cut, red-walled canyons; fantastically carved, multi-colored buttes and mesas; broad expanses of stony badlands. It is Indian Country, and has been for centuries; studded with extraordinary Anasazi ruins, the region is currently home to Zuni, Laguna and Acoma pueblos, and to the Navajo Nation, which controls some 16 million acres of reservation land.

But the face of the new West is visible here as well, decked out with the light-festooned "Christmas tree" pipelines of the gas fields, the slowly bobbing "grasshoppers" pumping oil. The northwest's barren San Juan Basin has turned out to be the fourth-largest natural gas field in the world; gas, coal, oil and uranium have transformed Farmington, Gallup and Grants into 20th century boom towns. The fact that several of these booms have lately gone bust seems, in this ancient land, part of a process; the wheel will keep turning and revival, of one kind or another, is imminent.

Northwestern New Mexico composes the southeast corner of the great Colorado Plateau, named for the river which, with its tributaries, has cut all those deep-walled canyons through masses of sedimentary rock. In New Mexico, this rock ranges in age from 330 to 2 million years old; the oldest of it is not exposed at the surface, but rather is draped in heavily folded drifts of pink, red, even orange sandstone, the characteristic, much-photographed rock of the region.

Perhaps the most distinctive geological feature of the area is the resource-rich San Juan Basin, named for the river that arcs across the state's northwest corner. Almost circular and 110 miles wide, the basin is made up of soft sandstones and siltstones ringed with harder sedimentary rocks that vault to the surface at its eastern edge as the hogback ridges footing the Brazos and Nacimiento Mountains. Here is Angel Peak, guardian of a collection of strangely shaped mesas, rugged cliffs and gashed canyons colored in banded shades of gray, blue, lavender, pink and tan. This sedimented rock—layers of mud piled atop layers of sand—was once washed by an inland sea.

Farther east, near Lumberton, the basin is marked by sheets of igneous rock called dikes, showing where magma once seeped through cracks in the earth's crust, then cooled. And dotting the western and southern edges of the basin are numerous volcanic necks, eroded cores of long-dead volcanos. The most famous of these is 1,500-foot-high Shiprock, near Farmington, a gothic-spired monolith sacred to the Navajo, who know it as *tae-bidahi*, "winged rock." According to legend, the Navajo, besieged by enemies, took refuge on the rock; suddenly it sprouted wings and sailed into the air, bearing them to safety.

South of the San Juan Basin lie the Zuni Mountains, their Precambrian granite exposed by millions of years of erosion. At their southern tip, the Zunis, in turn, nudge the swirling mass of lava flows and cinder cones known as El Malpais, the badland. At El Malpais National Monument, south of Grants, the twisted, grooved surfaces unfurl for miles, marked by lava caves and tubes created when molten lava flowed out from under its own cooling crust. Among the more remarkable of these formations are the Ice Caves, lava tunnels thick with blue-green ice that never melts, its eternal winter preserved by lava's insulating properties.

Some of the lava flows of El Malpais are only a thousand years old—quite young in geological terms—and their birth may well have been witnessed by the ancestors of local Indians; Indian story-tellers, in fact, speak of fire flowing from

STEPHEN TRIMBLE

TOM TILL

Above: Mt. Taylor, an extinct volcano, is the highest point in northwestern New Mexico.
Right: A Spaniard passing by in 1709 carved his name alongside the many others at Inscription Rock, now part of El Morro National Monument.

the earth and burning their forefathers' fields. Far older is Mount Taylor, an extinct volcano that reared forth some 4 million years ago. At 11,301 feet, Mount Taylor is the highest point in the area; the Navajo know it as *Tsoodzil*, the Turquoise Mountain, built by First Man as one of four sacred peaks defining the Navajo universe. On a more mundane level, its distinctive silhouette has provided relief to mountain-hungry travelers for a millenium.

Another kind of relief appears to the south, where a rain-fed pool laps at the base of a jutting sandstone bluff. With water so scarce locally, the pool long has been a magnet for travelers who, their thirst sated, then have allowed their attention to be drawn to the smooth expanse of soft stone presenting itself so temptingly, the proverbial blank slate. Local Indians, conquering Spaniards, westward-roaming Americans: all, for a thousand years, have been moved by a very human impulse and have postponed their travels long enough to scratch their names and occasionally a message or the dates of their passing on Inscription Rock, now part of El

Morro National Monument. Anasazi petroglyphs (picture writing) jostle pioneer notations; even Juan de Onate, New Mexico's ill-fated founder and first governor, could not resist: on his way back from an exploration of the Gulf of California, he stopped to write, "There passed by here Don Juan de Onate, from the discovery of the South Sea in 1605."

Before and after Onate, however, has been the Indian, the dominant force in northwestern New Mexico from time immemorial. The petroglyphs at Inscription Rock offer only a hint of the extraordinary Native American treasures to be found in the region, some—like the ruined cities of Chaco Canyon—ancient, others—like the Acoma pot you can see taking shape before your eyes—just being born.

The tumbled towns of the people the Navajo call Anasazi (the Ancient Ones) stud the area like precious gems, some hidden in sheltered canyons, others perched proudly on mesa tops. To the north, near Farmington, lies Aztec Ruins National Monument, misnamed by early American settlers, who thought they must have stumbled on cities constructed by the

THE NAVAJO NATION

STEPHEN TRIMBLE

The art of the Navajo jeweler.

Neither size (their reservation, overlapping New Mexico, Arizona and Utah, covers some 24,000 square miles) nor numbers (with 150,000 members, the tribe is the largest and fastest growing of any Indian group in America) led the Navajo to call themselves the Navajo Nation. The motivating factor came, rather, as a minor footnote to their tragic history. After being harried from their homeland in the mid-19th century, forced to take the harrowing Long Walk and incarcerated for years at the Bosque Redondo Reservation, the Navajo finally managed to win the right to return to their lands in the Four Corners area. A treaty was signed; its preamble stated that an agreement was being made between two sovereign powers. In their undaunted pride, the Navajo seized on this, claiming to be a nation within a nation, a position held to this day.

And today, it seems, they are right. The Navajo, with their enormous holdings, large population and mineral wealth, have built their own stores, restaurants, motels and shopping centers. They engage in logging, operate sawmills, oversee a utility authority and the massive irrigation projects of the Navajo Agricultural Products Industry. They have their own community colleges, their own police force and, supervising everything, a Tribal Council with 70 officials chosen by democratic election to represent the different areas of the reservation, called chapters. If these are not the activities of a nation, what, one might ask, are?

With all of this, the Navajo have remained closely tied to their traditions. The hogan—the eight-sided timber-and-mud dwellings utilized from their earliest nomadic days—is still the Navajo home of choice, although nowadays it may be adorned with a TV antenna, or stand beside a gleaming trailer. The matrilineal society—with each individual remaining a lifelong member of his or her mother's clan—endures. And, as with their Pueblo neighbors, religion continues to play a central role in the life of the Navajo. Curing ceremonials are particularly important, and with them, playing an integral part in the rites, the sand paintings that the Navajo have developed into a high art. Brilliantly colored and highly detailed, sand paintings most often depict events in the lives of the Holy People; they are usually destroyed before sunset on the day they are created.

More permanent examples of Navajo artistic expression may be found in finely woven rugs and magnificent silverwork, arts at which they have excelled for more than a century. Unfortunately, fewer and fewer Navajo are turning to these arts, finding that they can make more money at other jobs, often off the reservation.

This, sadly, seems to be something of a trend. For, although the reservation is rich, most Navajo people—like most Native Americans—live at or below the poverty level. Their lands, with all their beauty—and even with all their coal, oil and uranium—cannot support them all. The Navajo, nevertheless, retain their heritage of pride. Whatever befalls them—and they have survived conquistadors, missionaries and the U.S. Army—they remain a nation. Even more significantly, they remain *Dineh*. This is another thing the Navajo call themselves; it means, simply, The People.

Members of Zuni Pueblo's high school cross-country team work out in what must be one of the more starkly beautiful runner's environments in the nation.

of his family, the site was preserved intact until it could be purchased by the San Juan County Museum Association in 1967. While possibly not so dramatic as other ruins in the area, the Salmon Ruins are of particular interest because they are still in the process of being excavated and stabilized; there is always the potential of an important find being made right under one's nose!

It has already been learned that the stone and timbers for this 650- to 700-room complex may have been brought from as far away as southern Colorado. The fact that the Anasazi possessed neither wheel nor horse lends credence to the theory that such building materials must have been hand-carried along specially designed roads. And recent developments in satellite photography have, in fact, revealed the existence of just such a network of roads. Ramrod-straight, 20 to 30 feet wide, these boulevards (more than 1,200 miles of them) linked outlier communities—the pueblos of both the Salmon and Aztec Ruins among them—to one place, the center of the Anasazi world: Chaco Canyon.

Stone and silence: these are the hallmarks of Chaco Canyon today. But once, between 900 and 1150 A.D., a great civilization flourished there, 12 cities rising along the banks of a wash cutting through the narrow canyon, smaller hamlets clustering on the overlooking cliff-tops: urban housing, indeed, enough to domicile 7,000 souls in the boom years of the 11th century. Loveliest of all Chacoan ruins is that of Pueblo Bonito ("Pretty Town"), a five-story pueblo of nearly 800 rooms and 32 kivas. Its masonry was so finely fitted that mortar was seldom necessary; its walls stand, still sublime after a thousand years of wind, rain and sun. It is the Ninth Symphony of Anasazi architecture.

Brilliant architects and ingenious engineers, the Chacoans were also master potters and jewelers, farmers whose yield-per-acre (in spite of primitive irrigation methods in a dry land) rivalled modern returns, and astronomers exacting enough to construct solstice markers (visible at Chaco's Fajada Butte) precisely timing the equinoxes and solstices by which they measured their year. But perhaps their greatest achievement was their ability to sustain—for a while, at least—a strong sense of community. Despite the superficial similarities between Chacoan and modern urban life—high-density living, in particular—Chacoans did not suffer from

advanced civilizations of Mexico. One of the largest and best-preserved Anasazi ruins in the Southwest, Aztec is a horse-shoe-shaped pueblo of some 500 rooms built in the early 12th century. Its denizens were fine potters, and some beautiful examples of their work are on display at the adjacent museum, but Aztec Monument is most notable, perhaps, for its reconstructed Great Kiva. This simple ceremonial chamber, the only reconstruction of its kind in the United States, is in the classic circular shape, some 50 feet in diameter, its main floor eight feet below ground. Yet for all its simplicity, with its massively timbered roof and sculptural form, it has a kind of grandeur that links it quite naturally to the pyramid, the temple and the cathedral as an undeniably sacred structure.

Not far away, just west of Bloomfield, lies a very different kind of site, the Salmon Ruins. The remnants of an 11th-century pueblo, they were discovered in the 1800s by home-steader George Salmon; through Salmon's efforts, and those

NAVAJO WEAVING

In terms of their tribal history, the Navajo came late to weaving. Unknown to them in their primarily nomadic days, the craft was introduced to the Navajo only after they had migrated to northwestern New Mexico and taken up a more sedentary, agrarian-oriented life, probably after 1500. The Hopi may have been their first instructors, teaching the Navajo how to build looms and construct textiles on a large scale. Or other Pueblo groups may have brought the skill with them when they moved in with the Navajo at the time of the Spanish conquest. The Spanish, with their introduction of churro sheep, also provided the impetus for a dramatic leap forward in Native American textiles, which until then had relied on cotton and other vegetable fibers.

By the 18th century, the Navajo were the acknowledged masters of the craft, weaving in wool not only for their own use, but also for trade with the Pueblos and Spanish. Tools and techniques adopted from the Pueblos remained the same—the wide loom frame made of logs set into the ground, the figure-eight warping of the loom,

the method of weaving from the bottom up—but designs, previously limited to simple stripes, began to change with the application of the vivid Navajo imagination. Geometric shapes, diamonds, lozenges and zigzags were all introduced early on by the Navajo; by about 1820, these had been joined by symbolic representations of the elements, the seasons and times of day.

Navajo blankets of the mid-17th to the mid-19th centuries—the Classic Period—were prized for their dense weaving, which offered excellent protection from wind, rain and cold. Blankets were worn wrapped, sewn as dresses, used for sitting and sleeping, and hung in dwelling doorways to keep out the air, animals and spirits of the night. Best known of all Classic Period blankets are the stunningly simple, graphically brilliant chief's blankets.

Probably the greatest change to occur in Navajo weaving came as a result of the tribe's tragic imprisonment at the Bosque Redondo in the 1860s. Finally released to their old homeland, the Navajo had to try to take up their former lives with whatever was at hand. Their herds of churro sheep had been destroyed; no longer as readily available to them were the naturally colored white, gray, brown and black churro yarns. Instead, they were issued commercial Germantown yarns and cotton string in a wide variety of aniline-dye colors. Further, they had been influenced, during the years

JONATHAN A. MEYERS

at Bosque Redondo, by government-issue Saltillo serapes with their more complex designs.

The results were the explosive "eye-dazzlers," textiles of brilliant, extravagant colorings and serrated zigzag patterns. It has been speculated that the unsettling effect of these designs is reflective of the social and psychological upheaval experienced by the tribe during this time, known as the Transition Period of Navajo weaving.

By the beginning of the 20th century, Navajo weaving was a full-fledged commercial enterprise, often encouraged—and in some cases, actively guided—by such traders as Juan Hubbell and J.B. Moore, both of whom promoted the use of certain design motifs and advised their weavers to produce heavier rugs instead of the more traditional blankets. Among the many styles of this Modern Period (which continues to this day), perhaps the best known and most widely collected are the Two Grey Hills rugs,

The extraordinary quality of Navajo weaving has endured for three centuries.

originated at the New Mexican trading posts of Ed Davies and George Bloomfield. Unlike the equally prized "eye-dazzlers," they are subdued and elegant designs in a sombre spectrum of grey, black, brown, beige and white.

It should be noted that in the Navajo tribe—as in most Indian communities—women are the weavers. By tradition, they are limited to abstract designs and representations of non-living objects. Only men are allowed to create work representing human beings or animals, exceptions being made solely for textiles copied from sand paintings—this, presumably, because the original designs, the true art, were created by men. Perhaps because of the very limitations imposed on them, Navajo weavers—anonymous women artists—have, over the centuries, created work of dazzling rigor and imagination.

DAN PEHA

Above: Farmington, a town made possible by irrigation from the San Juan, Animas and La Plata rivers.

Facing page, top: *Enchanted Mesa figures in the lore of Acoma Indians, whose own mesa-top pueblo soars nearby.*
Bottom: *Acoma Pueblo, the renowned "Sky City," has looked out from its mesa for a thousand years.*

does little to discourage such feelings. We can only be trespassers there, offering, at best, a salute to the shades.

It seems fitting, somehow, this extraordinary reverence of Navajo for Anasazi. For although the Anasazi are ancestors of the Pueblo Indians, it is the Navajo who have become, in some sense, the Anasazis' inheritors in northwestern New Mexico. Their 16-million-acre reservation, the largest in the United States, blankets the Four Corners area; approximately one third of it is in New Mexico. It is mineral-rich land, the revenues from its oil, gas, uranium and coal providing the Navajo with schools, roads, dams and hospitals. The other side of the coin may be seen in the plumes of pollution drifting over Shiprock from the Four Corners Generating Plant. Driven by coal from the adjacent Navajo Mine, the country's largest open-pit operation, the plant supplies energy to several western states. At what cost? is the current, non-financial question.

The Navajo Nation (see page 49) has its governmental seat at Window Rock, Arizona; its primary trading centers, however, are in New Mexico. To the north is the trio of Aztec, Farmington and Bloomfield, sharing the fertile valley where the San Juan, Animas and La Plata Rivers join forces. Here red rock and silvery sage give way to 44,000 acres of lush green crops, the result of such successful experiments as the Navajo Irrigation Project. Here, too, are coal gasification plants and thermoelectric power projects, further products of the region's wealth of natural resources.

To the south is "America's most Indian off-reservation town," Gallup, which also bills itself as "the Indian Capital of the World." Once a stage stop, then (after 1881) a railroad town, Gallup is ramshackle but lively, an unrepentant, unreformed Western city crammed with "trading post" pawn shops that both glorify and take advantage of local Native Americans, the life's blood of the town's tourist trade.

This ambivalent relationship between Gallup and the Indian is evident everywhere, a two-sided coin turning up positive, then negative with almost equal regularity. On the positive side, for example, is the Inter-Tribal Indian Ceremonial, a five-day marathon of arts-and-crafts displays, sales and juried shows, parades, powwows, rodeos, Indian sports and games and truly spectacular Indian ceremonial dances—all of which Gallup plays host to on an annual basis. The Ceremo-

the anonymity and alienation that plague us today. Strong blood ties and a sense that everyday events were inextricably bound up with the spiritual (think of the ratio: 32 kivas to 800 rooms) helped; so also did the feeling (mostly lost to us today) that every individual played an essential part in the survival of the city.

Although it became a national monument in 1907 and was designated Chaco Culture National Historical Park in 1980, Chaco Canyon still may be reached only by unpaved and roundabout routes. There are those who believe this is for the best, that Chaco should not be exposed to the thundering herds of tourism, or to the desecrations that seem an inevitable part of modern life. The Navajo, on whose reservation Chaco lies, have made a practice of keeping strictly away from the ruins; the ghosts of the Anasazi, they feel, should not be disturbed. Certainly, despite its grandeur and undeniable beauty, the haunting, haunted atmosphere of Chaco Canyon nial, much of it held at nearby Red Rock State Park with its extraordinary outdoor arena ringed by startling formations of red sandstone, allows visitors the opportunity to see the truly dazzling array of Native talents and interests.

On the other hand, Gallup has a well earned reputation as "Drunk City," the place where Indians—not allowed to drink on the reservation—come to imbibe and, all too frequently, die; the local statistics for alcohol-related auto accidents are catastrophically high. Lately there has been growing pressure to outlaw the city's numerous drive-up liquor vendors, and a recent march from Gallup to Santa Fe—with crosses set out at the roadside to mark fatalities caused by drunkenness—focused considerable attention on a difficult and long-standing problem.

Although the 150,000-member Navajo tribe (the largest in the United States) dominates northwestern New Mexico, the pueblos of Zuni, Laguna and Acoma are also influential (see page 54). The Indians of Zuni and Acoma, moreover, have wielded that influence for several centuries longer than anyone else. The most westerly of all New Mexican pueblos, Zuni was the first to be visited by Spanish conquistadors; it was the Zuni village of Hawikuh (15 miles southwest of present-day Zuni) that was mistakenly believed to be one of the fabled Seven Cities of Gold. Acoma, the sublimely situated "Sky City" perched high on a mesa top east of Zuni, calls itself "the oldest continuously inhabited city in the United States"; its claim is a good one. When the conquistadors first laid eyes on the fortress pueblo in 1541, Acoma was already five or six centuries old, and although it was virtually destroyed by the Spaniards in 1599, it was almost immediately rebuilt on the same spot. Laguna is the newest of all Southwestern pueblos, settled in 1699 by refugees fleeing other pueblos after the Spanish reconquest. Situated hard by Interstate 40 just 50 miles from Albuquerque, this hilltop pueblo appears, nevertheless, untouched, basking quietly in the sun as it has done for nearly three centuries.

Unlike its sisters in the triumvirate of western pueblos, however, Laguna has always seemed oriented to the east. To the east lie the massifs of the Sandia and Sangre de Cristo Mountains. To the east is the great north-south string of major pueblos. And perhaps most significant of all is the eastward presence of the Mother River, the Rio Grande.

DAVID M. DENNIS

STEPHEN TRIMBLE

THE WESTERN PUEBLOS

KENT & DONNA DANNEN

Above: The construction of San Esteban del Rey mission church at Acoma Pueblo involved prodigious feats of labor: all building materials had to be hand-carried to the top of Acoma's 365-foot mesa.
Right: The graceful facade of the San Jose mission church, Laguna Pueblo.

RICHARD B. LEVINE

At some remove from the better known pueblos of the Rio Grande lie three of New Mexico's more fascinating Indian villages: the Western Pueblos of Zuni, Acoma and Laguna. Acoma is thought to be the oldest, Laguna is certainly the newest, and Zuni was the first to feel the heavy hand of the Spanish invaders.

Initially viewed in 1539 by Fray Marcos de Niza, the Zuni village of Hawikuh was mistakenly identified (from a distance, in the golden glow of the sun) as one of the legendary Seven Cities of Cibola. Coronado reached the village in 1540, attacked, and, for his pains, was rewarded with no gold, no bounty, no treasure-laden coffers. Accompanying priests were happier about their finds: potential souls for the saving.

Zuni warriors did not take kindly to Spanish Catholicism, however. Even today, tribal religion at Zuni remains particularly powerful, its rites and secrets jealously guarded. The Shalako Ceremonial, for example, considered by many to be the most beautiful and dramatic of all Indian ceremonials, is actually a year-long celebration of life; non-Indians, however, may view only one night of the rite, usually in late November or early December. And although the pueblo's mission church of Our Lady of Guadalupe has been recently restored, it seems significant that interior murals showing the Stations of the Cross also display large figures from the Zuni native religion.

With a reservation of 406,000 acres and a tribal population of about 4,500, Zuni has long relied on farming and stock raising for much of its income. Lately, however, the arts-and-crafts industry has blossomed; there are reportedly some 900 silversmiths at the pueblo—and with good reason. Zuni jewelry is justifiably famous, its painstaking "needlepoint" technique producing fine mosaic-like designs of turquoise, coral, mother-of-pearl and jet encased in silver.

Sadly for Zuni, the old village of Hawikuh (burned in 1670 by Apache raiders) lies abandoned, along with the ruins of several other ancient Zuni villages. The modern pueblo, built on the site of the old village of Halona, lies just 39 miles south of Gallup, abutting the sprawling town of Zuni, a mass of grocery stores, gas stations and arts-and-crafts shops. But the Zuni people have recently organized a tourist department to stimulate the industry on the reservation; one heartening by-product—at last, a good word for tourism!—is that plans are now afoot to restore the original, ancient pueblo.

The Sky City of Acoma, on the

other hand, sits where it has for more than a thousand years, atop a 365-foot-high sandstone mesa, some 65 miles west of present-day Albuquerque. The victim of an infamous Spanish siege in 1599, Acoma was burned, its population decimated. Survivors swiftly rebuilt, only to be subject to a new form of Spanish persecution: the building of the San Esteban Rey mission church under the dictatorial command of Franciscan priests.

Every bit of material used in the construction of the massive church had to be hand-carried to the mesa top, including the dirt for the adjacent cemetery and the 40-foot-long roof beams, each weighing several hundred pounds. Legend has it that the latter, brought from 40-mile-distant Mount Taylor, were never allowed to touch the ground. Somehow, the pain of all this toil is evident in the church, a brooding, if impressive edifice.

The past is, in fact, very much in evidence throughout Acoma, with its narrow streets, paving stones worn smooth by centuries of moccasined feet, and its tumble of stone and adobe dwellings clustered at cliff's edge. By general agreement, the tribe has allowed few modern conveniences at the pueblo: drinking water is carried from ancient stone catch basins, heating and cooking are done with wood.

Only 10 or 15 families of the 3,000-member tribe live permanently at the pueblo, maintaining the houses and church, operating the visitor center

and preparing for the feast days when all Acomas return to Sky City. Others live elsewhere on the 262,000-acre reservation, most working as stockmen or farmers, or in the arts-and-crafts industry. Acoma pottery—elaborately decorated with black-on-white or black-and-red-on-white designs, or all white with distinctive "fingernail" imprints—is some of the most beautiful of all pueblo ware.

New Mexico's newest pueblo, Laguna, has been described as a melting-pot of Southwestern Indian culture. Founded in 1699 by refugees from Cochiti, Santo Domingo and Zia pueblos fleeing the Spanish reconquest, Laguna was later to welcome settlers from Acoma, Zuni, Sandia, Jemez and even the Hopi Mesas in far-off Arizona. A rapidly swelling population caused the original settlement of Old Laguna to be joined by the satellite communities of Seama, Mesita, Encinal, Paguate and Paraje; these six villages today make up modern Laguna, lying some 50 miles west of Albuquerque.

The classic view of Old Laguna from I-40—the jumble of adobe homes tumbling down a sunny hillside—has been marred somewhat in recent years by the addition of modern homes and trailers. The presence of the open-pit Jackpile uranium mine has done little to improve the panorama. But the rose, pink and purple buttes still form a breathtaking backdrop, and the San Jose Mission, a spectacularly decorated church of mixed Indian and

TOM BEAN

Spanish influences, is well worth a visit.

Like their Navajo neighbors, the Lagunas are stockmen who have seen their lives transformed by the discovery of uranium on their 441,000-acre reservation. Marble quarries are also worked on Laguna land, while the satellite community of Mesita has recently inaugurated a 42,000-square-foot industrial complex. And while Laguna can boast fewer active artisans than other pueblos, the award-winning writer, Leslie Marmon Silko, wa raised there.

*Above: Laguna Pueblo sits in the sun below the blue reaches of Mount Taylor. **Below:** The stunningly intricate designs of modern Acoma pottery.*

VIRGINIA FERRERO

CHAPTER FOUR

NORTH-CENTRAL

RIO GRANDE HEARTLAND

DENNIS & MARIA HENRY

Above: Typically New Mexican cultural hodgepodge: a detail from the Spanish-Moorish-Hollywoodish facade of the Lensic Theatre, Santa Fe.

Facing page: Modern condos in Santa Fe reflect the continuing influence of Pueblo architecture.

This slice of New Mexico, bordered by two jagged prongs of the Southern Rockies and watered by the southerly-flowing Rio Grande, is probably the best known portion of the state—and the least understood. As ancient as the Anasazi ruins of Tyuonyi and as up-to-the-minute as the Atomic City of Los Alamos (the two towns, old and new, share the Pajarito Plateau), north-central New Mexico derives its character as much from the stylish capital city of Santa Fe as from the hidden Hispanic communities lost in time in the Sangre de Cristo Mountains.

The region offers some of the most pastoral, sheltering scenery in the state—and some of the most staggering, intense, human-obliterating panoramas in all of the Southwest. It is both an agricultural heartland, dotted with the orchards and neatly irrigated plots of small-crop farmers, and an historical one, rich with the lore of Indians and Hispanics, homesteaders and gunmen, the Santa Fe Trail and the Taos Art Colony. It is the contradictory embodiment of the state, blending the ancient and the modern, the everyday and the extraordinary in a rich and spicy brew.

Guarded on the north and east by the vaulting Sangre de Cristos and on the west by the broken and layered ranges of the Tusas, the Brazos and the Jemez Mountains, north-central New Mexico is roughly defined by the Rio Grande Rift, a long break in the earth's crust between two deep fault zones. The fault movements that created the rift began some 30 million years ago, accompanied by intense volcanic activity. Today, evidence of this activity may be seen in the numerous cinder cones, eroded volcanic necks and basalt lava flows that edge the region. One of the world's largest calderas—a collapsed volcano—is here, in the Jemez Mountains. Sixteen miles in diameter, edged with forests and

studded with ranches, the Jemez Caldera is also known as the Valle Grande: a broad, sun-soaked landscape revealing little of its violent birth.

More obvious exemplars of a thunderous volcanism are the region's numerous curving strings of lofty mountains; its stepped and eroded tablelands of delicately colored volcanic ash; and the high-piled, multi-layered lava flows that make up the Taos Plateau. Just north of Taos, where the Rio Grande has worn its way 650 feet down through the tuff of the plateau, it is possible to look into the river's gorge and see layer after layer of flow, firmly compacted and broken, here and there, by columnar joints that formed as the lava cooled. Geology is exposed and explained, there in the map-like walls of the Rio Grande Gorge.

Geographically speaking, the centerpiece of north-central New Mexico is the Rio Grande Valley, which, as it happens, is not a valley at all in the usual sense; that is, it was not cut by a river. Rather, the Rio Grande found and followed the trough already established there by the Rio Grande Rift; although rift was named for river, it was the rift that came first. Nevertheless, with its alternating cycles of sedimentary depositing and downcutting, the river has had a discernible effect on the rift. Many years of what geologist Halka Chronic calls "building and trenching, building and trenching" have created a series of step-like terraces along the rift edges; these are referred to as the Santa Fe group.

It has been along the margins of these terraces that, typically, first Indians, then Spaniards have settled, eager to take advantage not only of the Rio Grande's modest volume of precious water, but also of the rich alluvial soil developed on the site of old sand and gravel deposits. Unlike the Mississippi or Missouri rivers, the Rio Grande has not been a

DENNIS & MARIA HENRY

The state capitol in Santa Fe, with its circular, kiva-inspired architecture.

The first Spanish capital of New Mexico, San Gabriel, was established by Don Juan de Onate hard by the Rio Grande, near the present-day site of San Juan Pueblo. After Onate's colony failed, however, the Spanish crown ordered his replacement, Governor Pedro de Peralta, to found a new capital, more strategically located. Peralta picked a spot some 30 miles from the Rio Grande, nestled at the base of the Sangre de Cristos, with an unimpeded view of the Jemez Mountains to the west, the Ortiz and Sandia ranges far to the south. Legend has it that an ancient Tiwa pueblo once occupied the place, which local Indians poetically called "the dancing ground of the sun." There, 10 years before the Pilgrims landed at Plymouth Rock, Peralta—along with a few soldiers and their families—began to sketch out a low brown town, La Villa de Santa Fe.

Since then, four flags—those of Spain, Mexico, the Confederate States of America and the United States—have flown over Santa Fe. The city has witnessed the Spanish conquest, defeat and reconquest (still celebrated with the annual Fiesta de Santa Fe); the opening, heyday and decline of the Santa Fe Trail; the annexation by American forces; its own apotheosis as a major art colony; the arrival of nuclear scientists bound for Los Alamos and the Manhattan Project; and a post-war boom as tourists flooded in, drawn by the light, the air, cultural events beyond counting and the ambiance only several centuries of tumultuous history can provide.

Peralta's Palace of the Governors—the oldest public building in America in continuous use—still stands at the north edge of the city's nearly 400-year-old plaza; Indians now sell handcrafted pottery and jewelry beneath the *portal* (porch) of this building to which they once—in 1680, during the Pueblo Revolt—laid siege. Today the palace houses an excellent historical museum (the seat of government has been moved to an elegant, kiva-shaped capitol, erected in 1966), and teenage lowriders cruise around the plaza where the covered wagons and mule trains of the Santa Fe Trail once ended their arduous journey. In Santa Fe, this kind of historical juxtaposition (instant time travel, some have called it) is a commonplace.

A few blocks from the plaza, for example, just across the Santa Fe River (a glorified name for the little mountain creek along which the town was established), is the Barrio de

highway, a great mover of men or freight. More simply, it has been a life-giver in a dry land.

Along or near the river Coronado first found many of the ancestors of today's Pueblo Indians. Descendants, themselves, of the mysterious Ancient Ones of the Colorado Plateau, most had migrated to the Rio Grande Valley somewhere around 1300; by the time of the conquest, literally dozens of pueblos had been established in the area. Two centuries later, only 16 remained, with three others to the west. Cochiti, Isleta, Jemez, Nambe, Picuris, Pojoaque, Sandia, San Felipe, San Ildefonso, San Juan, Santa Ana, Santa Clara, Santo Domingo, Taos, Tesuque and Zia: these are the present-day pueblos of the Rio Grande, sole remnants of a bustling, burgeoning, vivid culture (see page 59: The Rio Grande Pueblos).

(continued on page 62)

THE RIO GRANDE PUEBLOS

STEPHEN TRIMBLE

Comanche dancers gather for a feast day, San Ildefonso Pueblo.

This gathering of 16 very different pueblos under one heading is done, it should be noted, as a matter of convenience. From Taos in the north to Isleta in the south to Jemez in the west, the people of these pueblos certainly share a common heritage, as well as the problems that face all Native Americans in the twilight of the 20th century. But they are also very different peoples, with different languages, their individual lifeways and customs a reflection of subtly differing attitudes towards life—of the earth and of the spirit.

It should be noted also that whole chapters—whole books—might be devoted to each pueblo. Not here, unfortunately; space and scope have limited us to only the briefest of sketches. The interested should make a point of visiting any or all of the New Mexican pueblos, each a repository of history, art, anthropology and the keenly spiritual.

According to legend, Cochiti Pueblo was founded some 600 years ago by immigrants from the Anasazi pueblo of Tyuonyi, principal ruin of Bandelier National Monument in the nearby Jemez Mountains (a similar claim is made by the Indians of San Ildefonso).

Located about 36 miles southwest of Santa Fe, Cochiti today is in the throes of transition. Although once extremely conservative, the pueblo recently became one of the first to enter into a business venture designed to bring income and jobs to its 28,000-acre reservation: the development of the resort community of Cochiti Lake. Cochiti artisans are well-known for their "storyteller" figurines, a recent innovation having little to do with the tradition of pueblo pottery, but charming nonetheless; the women surrounded by clinging children crafted by Helen Cordero are the foremost examples of this art. Cochiti men are equally famous for their excellent double-headed drums hollowed out of aspen or cottonwood.

The pueblo of Isleta, abutting the southern suburbs of Albuquerque, has the largest population of all New Mexican pueblos; most of these 3,000 tribal members work today in Albuquerque or nearby Belen. Despite the modernization of both its people and much of the pueblo itself, Isleta can still boast one of the most beautiful restored churches in the Southwest, the massive Mission of Saint Augustine, another claimant to the title of "oldest church in America." The pueblo is also famous for the quality of its bread, baked daily in the beehive-shaped *hornos,* outdoor ovens molded from adobe.

Forty-eight miles northwest of Albuquerque is Jemez Pueblo, set among the red-washed cliffs of the Jemez Mountains. Linked more than other pueblos to the traditions of neighboring Navajos, Jemez is also the sole pueblo to speak the Towa language. The 88,000-acre reservation continues to support many tribe members as farmers or stockmen; many others work in the arts and crafts trade. Thanks to potter Evelyn Vigil, traditional pottery has recently been revived at Jemez, utilizing natural colors, yucca leaf brushes and old-style pit-firing.

Nambe, a largely Hispanicized pueblo 21 miles north of Santa Fe, is currently involved in a program designed to revitalize its native crafts, which have languished in recent years. Most tribe members today work in nearby Espanola and Los Alamos, although a few still farm small fields on the 19,000-acre reservation. Every July 4, the pueblo hosts a popular celebration—complete with Indian dances—at the foot of the reservation's Nambe Falls.

Remote and tiny Picuris, located in mountainous country 20 miles south of Taos, has a current population hovering around 200; in the days before the Spanish conquest, it was considerably larger, "an aggressive, warlike community," according to writer Buddy Mays. Scraping a living from farming and stock-raising, modern inhabitants of the pueblo also are helping to restore the fascinating 700-year-old ruins of ancient Picuris. Picuris potters produce a micaceous

ABOVE: DENNIS & MARIA HENRY; BELOW: GEORGE WUERTHNER

even engaged in a pick-your-own farming operation, offering visitors the opportunity to gather corn, squash, melons and chiles directly from the fields.

San Felipe, located 28 miles north of Albuquerque, is one of the most conservative of all pueblos. No photography is permitted there, ever; few crafts, if any, are produced for the tourist trade; and the pueblo's handsome mission church, looming over a plaza worn several feet deep by centuries of ceremonial dancing, may be viewed only during services. Despite—or perhaps because of—this self-imposed isolation, the pueblo's Feast Day each May 1 is one of the most spectacular of all Indian ceremonials.

The work of ceramic artist Maria Martinez and her husband Julian has brought enduring fame to the pueblo of San Ildefonso, 24 miles northwest of Santa Fe. Their burnished black pottery with matte black designs is, today, virtually priceless, and has served as splendid inspiration for the dozens of potters currently working out of the pueblo. Set against the beautiful tableland beneath the Pajarito Plateau, San Ildefonso retains its striking appearance in large part thanks to a strict tribal construction code; in 1957, a church of recent vintage was unceremoniously demolished to make way for a detailed replica of the 17th-century original occupant of the site.

Considered the most progressive of all the pueblos, San Juan (also highly Hispanicized) is the headquarters for

utility ware, one of the few types of Indian pottery considered safe for cooking; in fact, it is said that food cooked in a Picuris pot has added flavor.

Reduced almost to extinction, the highly Hispanicized pueblo of Pojoaque has nonetheless managed to reestablish itself; it now has a tribal council and recently reinstated observance of its feast day. Located 16 miles north of Santa Fe, Pojoaque has a small commercial complex at the junction of the Santa Fe-Los Alamos highway, from which it derives most of its tribal income.

Sandia Pueblo, just 14 miles from Albuquerque at the foot of the Sandia Mountains, has capitalized on its metropolitan location by encouraging tourism. The pueblo leases land for the Sandia Peak Tram, has built an arts-and-crafts center where work of many pueblo artisans is sold, and has

the Eight Northern Pueblos Council, an all-Indian group promoting economic, educational and cultural benefits for its members. Its 1,400 tribal members farm much of the reservation's 12,000 acres (located 29 miles north of Santa Fe), lease land to a lumber company and operate a large bingo parlor. They are also overseeing the renovation of some 100 historically significant pueblo buildings, and participating in an arts and crafts revival that has produced fine incised pottery, coral and turquoise jewelry, leather and bead work, baskets and weaving.

Thirty miles northwest of Albuquerque lies Santa Ana Pueblo, which may not be visited except on special feast days. Most tribal members live in farming communities near Bernalillo, returning to the pueblo only for the occasional ceremonial. Nonetheless, Santa Ana is known for its traditional polychrome pottery, recently rescued from near oblivion by Endora Montoya; she revived the craft, teaching it to a number of Santa Ana women and helping to organize a cooperative to market their wares. Nearby Coronado State Monument preserves the ruins of an ancient pueblo built, according to legend, by ancestors of present-day Santa Anans.

The people of Santa Clara, 30 miles northwest of Santa Fe, administer the magnificent Puye Cliff Ruins, their ancestral home. Perched on a forested ledge of the Pajarito Plateau, with sweeping views of the Sangre de Cristo

Mountains, Puye is one of the most stunningly located Anasazi sites in the Southwest—and never more so than during Santa Clara's annual July ceremonial, when the soaring Eagle Dance is performed on the cliffs, with a backdrop of tumbled stone. Santa Clara artisans are excellent potters, producing an exquisite burnished and incised black ware; two Santa Clara painters, Pablita Velarde and her daughter, Helen Hardin, have also won international recognition with their depictions of Indian life.

STEPHEN TRIMBLE

Another extremely conservative pueblo, Santo Domingo is highly traditional in its village life, and neither encourages nor welcomes tourism. Santo Domingo artisans (many of whom sell their work beneath the portal of the Governor's Palace in Santa Fe) are some of the foremost jewelers of the Southwest; their strings of heishi—tiny, flat discs of bone, shell and turquoise—are particularly fine. Potter Robert Tenorio has also done much to revive traditional black-and-cream-on-red ware.

Maintaining a hotbed of resistance until well into the 19th century, the people of Taos Pueblo have held onto their stubborn individuality and fierce pride to this day: it was Taos Indians who beat the U.S. government after a 50-year battle, winning back their sacred site at Blue Lake; it is Taos Indians who steadfastly refuse to allow electrification of their beautiful multi-storied pueblo; it is Taos Indians who stick to farming and stock-raising, caring little, it seems, about the world of the tourist

and big business enterprise. Taos Indians are also particularly distinctive in appearance: because of their long contact with Plains Indians, they have adopted such customs as wearing long cloth-wrapped braids and draped blankets, unknown among other Pueblo peoples. Taos artisans produce a small amount of pottery, drums and leather and bead work; their dances are some of the most beautiful, and their dancers some of the most skilled, in all the pueblos.

Tesuque, a small pueblo 10 miles north of Santa Fe, has recently experienced a revival in the making of its unique pottery: red and gray-brown vessels with figures of animals—lizards, frogs, snakes and such—molded to their sides. The Tesuque Indians also administer the campground at nearby Camel Rock, a well known landmark along the Santa Fe-to-Taos highway, and operate a booming bingo parlor.

Zia Pueblo, perched on a mesa-top 36 miles northwest of Albuquerque, is

DENNIS & MARIA HENRY

an old and crumbling village of conservative bent. Its potters are exceptionally talented; their polychrome ware decorated with bird and animal motifs and stylized flowers, is energetic, yet delicate. Perhaps the best-known Zia design is the ancient sun symbol that appears on New Mexico's state flag, representing "perfect friendship."

Above: The sculptural beauty of adobe is evident in this stepped wall and domed horno *(outdoor bake oven) at Taos Pueblo.*
Left: Santa Ana Pueblo potter Endora Montoya displays her work.
Facing page, top: Native Americans selling their wares in the shade of a portal, Old Town, Albuquerque.
Bottom: The simple adobe church at Tesuque Pueblo.

61

Above: The lights of Santa Fe pale beneath the encompassing brilliance of a Southwestern sunset.

Facing page: Penitente cross erected on a ridge near the ancient mountain hamlet of Truchas.

at Loretto, a massive hotel that city fathers allowed to be built right on the grounds of the exquisite 19th-century neo-Gothic Loretto Chapel; built, however, in great good taste, in Pueblo style, with the additional proviso that the chapel be protected in perpetuity.

Nothing is perfect, and even Santa Fe has its eyesores: Cerrillos Road, the banks of condominiums that ring the city, the gimcrack shops that cater to the seasonal hordes of tourists flooding the town. Yet it is still possible, here, to lose oneself in an atmosphere far from the hurly-burly of our own century; to dine in a former convent and shop in a former hacienda; to sit peacefully in a thick-walled chapel as the privileged light of northern New Mexico floods past the windows' deep jambs; and everywhere, to be nourished by the broad views of mesa and mountain that are the town's most basic charm, timeless and compelling.

Santa Fe still can be entered by the Old Santa Fe Trail, the same narrow winding track—now paved—followed by 19th-century traders and travelers coming in to the shelter of the city from the perilous eastern plains. And, moving north, one can leave by yet another storied path: the fabled High Road to Taos. There is another, faster way to get to the magical town on its mile-high mesa: a highway cutting through the Espanola Valley, often running parallel to the Rio Grande, climbing past the orchard-shaded towns of Alcalde, Velarde and Pilar. But the High Road offers something more than speed and scenery: a journey into New Mexico's Hispanic past.

Nambe, Chimayo, Cordova, Truchas, Las Trampas, Penasco: the lilting names of the mountain villages are the poetry of the High Road. Once considered so isolated that banishment to them was appropriate punishment for the most heinous crimes, these hamlets have survived centuries of Apache raids, Pueblo rebellions, Anglo land grabs and comparatively simple storm, flood and drought. Today they are outposts of the modern world: remote, rustic, Spanish to the bone. Chimayo is a holy center, its Santuario known as the Lourdes of America (see sidebar: Chimayo and Hispanic Folk Arts); Cordova is famous for its woodcarvings, Truchas for its spectacular mountain views, Las Trampas for a superb Spanish Colonial church. All are, perhaps, most remarkable for being pockets of the past, their look (barring the occasional

Analco, a district of a few narrow streets and alleyways draped in lilac and wisteria, its high-walled adobe houses looking like stage sets for a Catalan operetta. Once the area reserved to house the Indian servants of early Spanish colonists, the barrio is—next to the plaza—the oldest section of Santa Fe. Yet within steps of what boosters claim as "the oldest church in America" and "the oldest house in America" (neither actually is), are bustling hotels, ritzy galleries, tatty souvenir shops and chic restaurants. Santa Fe absorbs it all; somehow, the crazy mix works.

If the past is palpably present everywhere in Santa Fe, it is in large part thanks to a caring populace that has supported such measures as the 1957 ordinance requiring all new construction in the town's older areas to be architecturally in keeping with local style. This has been done, occasionally, with what can only be called a cagey appreciation of the advantages of controlled growth. A prime example is the Inn seemingly inevitable mobile home), language, customs and overall ambiance as antique as any local santo or reredo.

And then, at last, the goal: Taos, set dramatically on its volcanic plateau with the peaks of the Sangre de Cristos rearing up against the northern and eastern skyline. Taos, by which D.H. Lawrence (among a legion of others) was so bewitched that he wrote, "So beautiful, God! so beautiful! Those that have spent morning after morning alone there pitched among the pines above the great proud world of desert will know almost unbearably how beautiful it is, how clear and unquestioned is the might of the day...the heart is sacrificed to the sun and the human being is left stark, heartless, but undauntedly religious."

This kind of sincere if overheated rhetoric is typical of the response to Taos, a place that has been, traditionally, hard to get to, difficult to survive in and yet easy to love. Lawrence spent a mere three summers at a ranch overlooking the Taos Valley (a ranch given to him by his patron, another Taos fanatic, the indefatigable Mabel Dodge Luhan), but after his death in France, his wife, Frieda, brought his ashes back to New Mexico and had them interred on the mountainside with that vast view of high desert mesa opening out below. This act implies a devotion completely comprehensible to those who have seen Taos, and felt its very individual charm.

Raving about that charm is one thing; pinpointing it is more difficult, and has left far better writers than this one floundering. Mabel Dodge Luhan felt that, for those living in Taos, "there is an extrasensory life in our surroundings, observable, but not understood." This indefinable feeling of power in the landscape goes beyond geography to the mystical, and perhaps accounts for reiterated descriptions of a sky "so brilliant that it vibrates," of light that is "spiritual," of a general atmosphere "privileged in the way of ancient Greece."

First to share in this privileged atmosphere were the Taos Indians, who came to the area about a thousand years ago, establishing their strikingly beautiful multi-storied pueblo around 1300 A.D. Legend maintains that the Indians were led to the spot by an eagle, who dropped a feather on each side of a stream; these feathers marked the sites of the Pueblo's North and South houses, five-storied communal dwellings built of adobe on either bank of the Rio Pueblo.

Separated from other Rio Grande Pueblos by the moun-

KENT & DONNA DANNEN

DENNIS & MARIA HENRY PHOTOS

Above: Wheeler Peak, New Mexico's highest mountain, soars over an upland ranch near Eagle Nest. Right: The striking adobe architecture of centuries-old Taos Pueblo reflects the pyramidal shapes of its mountain backdrop.

tains, the Taos Indians were threatened on the plains by their proximity to the belligerent Apache. When the Apache didn't raid, however, they traded; this was the beginning of Taos' cultural diversity, a tradition that would continue with the arrival first of the Spanish, then the Americans. Initial relations between the Spanish and the Indians were friendly, but when missionaries persisted in their efforts to Christianize the already deeply religious Indians, resistance mounted; the Pueblo Revolt of 1680 erupted first at Taos. Nearly two centuries later, Hispano-Indian resistance to American rule also exploded into violence, with the Taos Rebellion of 1847; the town's reputation as an untamed place of hotheads and free-thinkers seems, at least on occasion, justified.

After the reconquest, Taos—the Pueblo, the original Spanish settlement of Don Fernando de Taos and the farming community of Ranchos de Taos—began to develop as an important center for frontier commerce. Informal business went on year-round, while twice a year, a well organized trade fair saw a brisk business in buffalo hides, beaver pelts, grain, flour, baskets, blankets, pottery, horses, bullets, Indian captives and *aguardiente,* a potent whiskey known as Taos Lightning. On these occasions, the town would be bursting with Indians of both Pueblo and nomadic tribes, Spanish farmers and soldiers, French beaver trappers and fur traders and, by the mid-19th century, American trappers, prospectors, mountain men, traders and adventurers pouring over the Santa Fe Trail.

The wares may have changed, but otherwise this scene is not too different from what may be viewed on the streets of Taos today, at the height of the summer tourist season. With the establishment, just after the turn of this century, of the Taos Society of Artists, the town entered the modern world as a renowned center for the arts. Today, with a population of only around 5,000, Taos is nevertheless home to numerous festivals and arts oriented events, can boast an array of nearly 100 art galleries, and is a mecca for tourists.

The seductive beauty of the town has been, and continues to be, both a blessing and a curse. Tourism often has kept Taos alive, not negligible in a place where farming, the principal occupation, exists mostly on a subsistence level. The Taos Ski Valley, for example, founded in the late 1940s, has developed into an internationally popular resort, providing

CHIMAYO & HISPANIC FOLK ARTS

DENNIS & MARIA HENRY

Legend tells us that early in the 19th century, a Penitente brother, Bernardo Abeyta, was making his penance in a field on the outskirts of the little mountain village of Chimayo. The rite was interrupted by the sudden appearance of a brilliant light, shining forth from a hole in the ground. With his bare hands, Abeyta dug at the spot, uncovering an exquisitely carved and painted crucifix. Abeyta took the crucifix to the local priest, who had it moved to a church in the villa of Santa Cruz. The next morning, the crucifix had vanished from its niche in the church altar, only to reappear in the hole in the Chimayo field. Twice more, it was carried back to Santa Cruz; twice more, it reappeared in the hole. By this time, everyone understood that the crucifix wished to remain in Chimayo. The renowned Santuario de Chimayo was built to house and honor the crucifix of Our Lord of Esquipulas; the earth from the hole—also guarded by the Santuario—began to show significant healing properties; and today Chimayo is known as the Lourdes of America.

Each year, thousands of pilgrims journey to the Santuario to partake of the *tierra bendita* (blessed earth), which is believed to cure everything from arthritis to sadness. Evidence of the many cures apparently effected by the "magic mud" is on display in the chambers adjacent to the main chapel: row after row of cast-off crutches and braces, testimonial letters and photographs. At Holy Week, the steady stream of pilgrims increases to a flood, some coming hundreds of miles, often on foot, occasionally carrying crosses or shuffling the last few miles on their knees.

Sometimes lost in all the human procession is an appreciation of the remarkable beauty of the Santuario itself. Its pastoral setting, primitive but elegant architecture, and the intensely expressive quality of its *santos* (carved wooden saints) and *reredo* (altar screen) combine to make the Santuario as a whole a work of art, both serene and vivid in its integrity.

Santos and reredos, along with *bultos* (carved wooden statues, not necessarily representing saints), *retablos* (paintings or carvings made on flat wooden tablets) and *muertos* (the "death carts"—startling representations of grim-visaged, skeletal figures driving wooden carts—most often associated with the Penitentes) were typical expressions of the *santeros*, religious image-makers who worked in a distinctively New Mexican style. The work of the santeros was so intense—and occasionally painful—that it was often banned by the official Catholic Church, which preferred a more delicate, homogenized religious art; Archbishop Lamy, in particular, was notoriously opposed to the display of santos. Yet the woodcarver's art has endured and flourished in New Mexico, nurtured by its long and flamboyant tradition. The late Patrocinio Barela of Taos and several members of Cordova's Lopez family are renowned modern santeros, while such artists as Felipe Archuleta and Jimbo Davila (among others) have taken local traditions in a new direction with their delightfully humorous carvings of animals and reptiles.

Since the early 1800s, Chimayo has also been the center for another noted Hispanic art: weaving. Two Mexican master weavers, the brothers Ricardo and Juan Bazan, brought their techniques north to colonial New Mexico, teaching the locals to use homespun wool and vegetable dyes in the production of softly-colored blankets and rugs. Although the craft declined after the introduction of mass-produced commercial goods, it was revived during the general artistic renaissance of the 1920s, and the Chimayo or Rio Grande blankets produced today by such textile artists

The interior of the Santuario de Chimayo, with its simply plastered and painted walls, lofty log-beamed ceiling, carved wooden saints and magnificent altar screen, is a supreme example of Hispanic art.

as the Ortega, Cordova and Trujillo families are of extremely high quality.

Other Hispanic arts currently enjoying a new popularity are the extravagantly embroidered *colchas* (bedspreads) and *sabanillas* (altar cloths) with their swirling, brightly-hued floral motifs; the frames, lanterns, candleholders and crosses decorated with braids, spirals, vines, birds and stars by the region's talented tinsmiths; and such folk plays as *Las Posadas* and *Los Pastores,* Nativity stories staged by many communities at Christmas time.

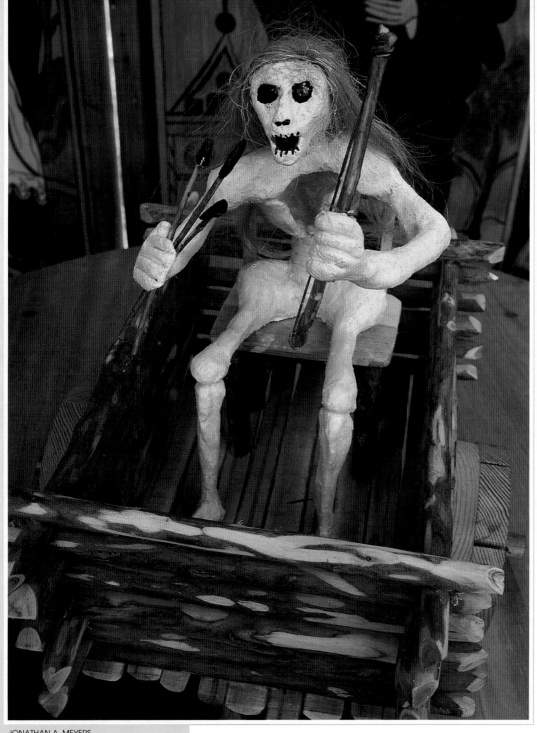

JONATHAN A. MEYERS

jobs for many Taoseños who might otherwise have had to leave the area. Yet, others argue, is it right for a man whose family has been farming in the Taos Valley for three centuries to be forced to take a job setting pitchers of ice-cold martinis along the ski runs for thirsty schussers? At the very least, it is hard to ignore the irony of such a situation.

Such situations are more and more the norm these days, not just in Taos, but in the rest of New Mexico as well—which makes what happens in Taos particularly worth watching.

Taos County is one of the poorest in the nation; it is difficult to look askance when developers move in, offering jobs. It is equally hard to blame people with families to care for when they sell off their farmlands for condominium projects or shopping malls. But unchecked development is making its mark on the face of Taos. Ten years ago, you could stand in the center of town and, turning, see where town ended and farmland and mesa began. Now, to the south, an ugly strip of fast-food joints and automotive shops trails off like a tail of tin cans.

Is this the face of the future? Better not to count Taos out too quickly. It is, after all, a place of miracles. A painting of Christ at Ranchos de Taos's sculpturally buttressed mission church appears, at times, to carry a cross; at other times, no cross is visible. The Taos Indians, despite enormous pressure, steadfastly refuse to allow electricity or running water to be installed at the pueblo, thus ensuring its preservation as a massive historic artifact...and as their ancestral home. And above it all, the sturdy, soaring shape of Taos Mountain endures, blue as heaven, blue as the scented piñon smoke rising from all the adobe chimneys of the durable, magical town it guards.

West of Taos Mountain, past the great gash of the Rio Grande Gorge, lies the region's north country, ridged by a backbone of two parallel mountain ranges: the Tusas and Brazos. The Sangre de Cristos run right on up into Colorado very near here, and the north wind whipping down through the passes has scoured the granite and volcanic tuff of the smaller ranges into strange, sculptural forms, their pinkish rock contrasting sharply with the piney greens of the blanketing Carson National Forest.

It was the forest which first drew people to this part of New Mexico; by 1870, a thriving sawmill was in operation at a village appropriately dubbed Slabtown. A few years later, the same village, now renamed Chama, became the leading town in Rio Arriba County when a narrow-gauge railroad line was run through it, connecting mines in Colorado with points south and west. Today New Mexico and Colorado jointly own and operate 64 miles of this line as the Cumbres & Toltec Scenic Railroad, a puffing steam engine and restored rolling stock running between Chama and Antonito, Colorado. The sturdy little train crosses 10,015-foot-high Cumbres Pass and winds through dramatic Toltec Gorge; the trip is especially beautiful in fall, when shimmering aspens flood the mountainsides with streams of molten gold.

The Chama area is a paradise for hunters and anglers, its forests alive with elk and deer, its lakes, streams and the Chama River stuffed with trout: rainbow, brook and German brown. Also benefitting from this natural abundance has been nearby Dulce, the capital and principal town of the 750,000-acre Jicarilla Apache Reservation. Once depending on the uncertain income provided by ranching and the sale of oil leases, the Jicarilla, like their Navajo neighbors to the west, are increasingly turning to tourism, operating campgrounds at Dulce and Mundo lakes, both excellent trout waters. A modern lodge at Stone Lake, meanwhile, offers guided hunts for the elk, deer, bear, wild turkey and waterfowl that inhabit the reservation's rolling, piñon-dotted hills and stately spruce forests.

The Chama River, flowing south, soon meanders out of forested lands and into the sun-soaked, red-rocked landscape around the old genizaro village of Abiquiu. Here, amidst some of the most spectacular scenery in northern New Mexico, the Spanish colonial government established a settlement for *genizaros* of mixed blood who were either Spanish prisoners or captives of other Indian tribes recently ransomed and released from slavery, or who adopted a Hispanic lifestyle. By the end of the 18th century, Abiquiu was the site of an important trade fair, and a stop on the Old Spanish Trail, which led west to a tiny coastal hamlet called Los Angeles.

But Abiquiu and its environs truly came into their own two centuries later, as subject of and inspiration for artist Georgia O'Keeffe, one of the greatest American painters of our age. In canvas after canvas, she immortalized the land she loved and lived in for the last 40 years of her long life: towering

KENT KRONE

red cliffs of worn and weathered sandstone, dazzling white cliffs thickly sandwiched with gypsum, rosy rockbeds capped with darker basalt, and over all, the high, clear turquoise sky shedding a light of almost unbelievable radiance.

Tucked along the base of the cliffs so often depicted by O'Keeffe (who once said of a nearby mountain, "It's mine. God told me he'd give it to me if I painted it often enough.") are deposits of Triassic rock thick with dinosaur fossils. Over a thousand specimens of *Coelophysis*—the oldest known dinosaur, recently designated the state fossil of New Mexico—have been unearthed there, many near Ghost Ranch, O'Keeffe's summer home. There, also, is the Ghost Ranch Living Museum, a fascinating blend of exhibits on local wildlife,

DENNIS & MARIA HENRY

Above: A bull elk bugles from a hillside near Chama.
Left: The Rio Chama tinges the rocky landscape with green near Abiquiu.

Facing page: A muerto, or "death cart," crafted by John Gonzales. Such images are important reflections of Penitente beliefs.

67

The ruins of Tsankawi, an unexcavated late Anasazi village, look out over the Sangre de Cristo Mountains from Bandelier National Monument.

ratory, devoted to nuclear research for both national defense and peaceful application. At its boundaries is Bandelier National Monument, containing—in narrow, sunlit Frijoles Canyon—the ruins of an Anasazi pueblo, Tyuonyi.

Named for Adolph Bandelier, the Swiss-American scholar who, at the end of the 19th century, made an extensive survey of prehistoric ruins in the area, Bandelier covers about 50 square miles, 90 percent of which is virtually undisturbed wilderness. Shadowy caves and dusty canyons, deep gorges and dense pine forests all exist here as they did when the Anasazi were their only human inhabitants.

The Monument's most accessible ruins (Bandelier is studded with them, including Tsankawi, a remarkable unexcavated village situated on a high mesa some 11 miles north of Frijoles Canyon) are those of Tyuonyi, lying along—and above—the Rito de los Frijoles (Bean Creek), named for the pueblo-dwellers' primary crop. Over millenia, this mountain-rising stream has cut the deep gorge that is Frijoles Canyon from the volcanic tuff: tawny pink, ashy rock full of holes eroded by wind and rain.

The pueblo peoples who lived here made good use of this rock, quarrying what they needed for masonry houses built around a plaza and circular kiva on the canyon floor below. Alternatively, working with tools of harder stone, they would gouge their houses right out of the solid cliff. Called talus houses, these extend for some two miles along the north wall of Frijoles Canyon, irregularly terraced, one to three stories high. Such dwellings still seem, somehow, to burst with life: their floors still scattered with pueblo pottery shards, their walls still scratched with pictographs that are charming, funny and occasionally obscene, their roofs still blackened by the smoke of Anasazi fires. All this, just a few hundred yards from a laboratory where men are contemplating new and better ways to put an end to the earth the Pueblos still regard as sacred.

The Atomic Age and the Ancient Ones: this is the kind of juxtaposition novelists would be sneered at for inventing. Yet it is perfectly typical of New Mexico—and of the north-central region, in particular. Here, old and new can exist side by side, naturally significant, each lending a deeper resonance to the other.

paleontology and conservation, administered by the U.S. Forest Service.

Farther south, between the rising peaks of the Jemez Mountains and the Rio Grande, the land crimps and folds into a broad expanse of step-like mesas, some—like the famous Black Mesa, sacred to the San Ildefonso and Santa Clara Indians—of dark-colored basalt, others of pale-hued sand and gravel. These buff, salmon, peach, rose and even violet-colored, wildly beautiful *barrancas* sweep up to the foot of the Pajarito (little bird) Plateau, a mass of pink, thickly consolidated volcanic tuff poised at the base of the Jemez Mountains.

There, in splendid isolation, lie two cities, modern and ancient jostling each other, cheek by jowl. The atomic city of Los Alamos, founded in 1943 to accommodate the Manhattan Project, is still home to the Los Alamos Scientific Labo-

PUEBLO POTTERY

Perhaps the surest indication of the Pueblo Indians' lasting devotion to their cultural heritage may be seen in the intricate designs, sculptural shapes and finely burnished surfaces of their pottery. The prize-winning, attention-grabbing, money-making pots of today are made in the same way as the centuries-old utilitarian vessels of their Anasazi and Mimbres ancestors. The best are made, moreover, with an acknowledgment of the spirit behind the creative force rare in any modern artistic endeavor. Teresita Naranjo, member of a multi-generational family of Santa Clara potters, puts it this way: "God is always with me. He is the Potter. He molds my life, and I mold the potteries."

Pueblo potters (until the last few decades, almost exclusively women) do not use the potter's wheel; their work is crafted entirely by hand, using the coil method. Long sausages of clay (often dug and mixed locally) are coiled up from a clay base until the desired height is reached; when coiling is finished, both the interior and exterior of the pot are smoothed, most frequently with a stone shaped for the purpose. Cracks or imperfections are filled in with slip, an almost liquid mixture of clay and water; colored slips may be used to tint the pot's surface. Carving or further burnishing may take place; then the pot is pit-fired and, often, decoratively painted.

There are, of course, many variations on this basic process. Carbon paint or mineral paint may be utilized for different effects; the method of firing also varies according to the desired result. It is from these differences that the extraordinary variety of modern Pueblo pottery derives.

Along with other native New Mexican arts, pottery experienced a decline with the introduction of manufactured products to the area around the turn of the century. Similarly, the Pueblos participated in the astonishing artistic revival of the 1920s, a revival that has continued at full steam to this day. To a great extent, that revival was stimulated by the work of Maria Martinez of San Ildefonso. Inspired by shards of Anasazi pottery discovered in an archaeological dig, Maria (aided by her husband, Julian Martinez) developed the matte-black-on-polished-black style that won her international fame. In 1925, Maria began signing her work, an unheard-of innovation that reflected the new appreciation of her work as art.

San Ildefonso potters continue to be innovators. Rose Gonzales introduced intaglio techniques to the

STEPHEN TRIMBLE

Pecos glazeware by Evelyn Vigil at Pecos National Monument.

pueblo in the 1930s; later, Blue Corn revived the languishing polychrome style. Popovi Da, son of Maria and Julian Martinez, developed a firing technique to produce a black and sienna ware, and his son, Tony Da, has maintained the avant-garde tradition of his family by decorating his work with inlaid turquoise.

At Santa Clara, the Tafoya/Naranjo potting dynasty has produced stunning carved and burnished vessels, while at Acoma, the women of the Lewis and Chino families make a thin, delicate white ware decorated with intricate geometric or animal designs adapted from ancient Mimbres pots.

The storyteller figurines of Helen Cordero and other Cochiti potters are a less traditional but charming variation on other Pueblo themes.

The dynamism of Pueblo potters is one of their most astonishing characteristics. Yet even as they continue to grow and change—offering inspiration, these days, even to such outstanding non-Indian exponents of the art as Rick Dillingham and Juan Hamilton—they remain rooted in their collective past, when beautiful things were made for simple purposes: to carry water, to store grain, to go about the business of everyday life.

69

NORTHEAST
ALONG THE SANTA FE TRAIL

KENT & DONNA DANNEN

Above: At Fort Union
National Monument.

Facing page: Rabbit Ear
Mountain, floating in the
distance: a major landmark on
the Santa Fe Trail.

Where the rugged Rockies edge the New Mexico-Colorado border in the northeastern quadrant of the state, there is a narrow gap, a so-called "low point" amidst the jagged peaks, the air at its 8,000-foot summit wind-washed and thin. Plains Indians, travelers on the Santa Fe Trail and finally the railroad builders: all negotiated the steep and perilous ascent to the top of Raton Pass, and were well rewarded. There, spread before them like a velvety tapestry, were the long, shimmering plains of northeast New Mexico, dotted with the blue cones of sleeping volcanoes.

Still the northeastern gateway to the state, Raton Pass sits amidst volcanic ramparts, their sedimentary rock thickly encrusted with basalt lava flows 3.5 to 7.2 million years old. Layers of sandstone and shale seamed with coal drop down to the Raton Basin; once, they formed the shores of a shallow inland sea ringed with mudflats and sandbars, marshes and swamps. The dark gray Pierre shale (named for Pierre, South Dakota) was deposited as mud on the floor of this sea; it is studded with well preserved fossilized remains of cephalo-pods, sharks and marine reptiles. Light-brown Dakota sand-stone, porous and permeable, retains water and serves as an aquifer for the basin. Today, the scenically situated town of Raton lies on these layers of rock, near the head of the Canadian River Valley.

Founded as Willow Springs, Raton was the first New Mexican stop on the Mountain Branch of the Santa Fe Trail, which forked in western Kansas, leaving travelers with two alternatives for continuing their journey. The Cimarron Cutoff, to the south, was 85 miles shorter and ran through less rugged (though often waterless) terrain, but it was shadowed by the ever-present threat of attack by hostile Indians. The

Mountain Branch, on the other hand, turned north into the Colorado Rockies where travel could be more demanding, but the route was protected by several forts, and many Trailers were willing to swap a swift trip for a safe one (see page 72: The Santa Fe Trail).

The appeal of the Trail's Mountain Branch increased after the Civil War when "Uncle Dick" Wootton—mountain man, Indian fighter, trader and stockman—purchased a ranch from the Maxwell Land Grant that included the Raton Pass, then proceeded to fell trees, blast rock and build bridges, thus improving 27 miles of the trail route. Wootton set up a toll-gate at the New Mexico-Colorado border, charging the then-princely sum of $1.50 per wagon for passage; those who wished to pass without paying were likely to meet Uncle Dick's "toll collector": a long-barrelled shotgun.

When the Atchison, Topeka & Santa Fe Railroad came through in 1879, the company bought Wootton's toll road and transformed the little watering hole of Raton into a railroad boom town. Ranching and coal-mining brought further benefits, and by the turn of the century, Raton was a thriving community rich with late-Victorian atmosphere and architecture. Remnants of that opulence are preserved today in the town's five-block historic district, highlighted by such gems as the massive stone Palace Hotel (housing an elegant restaurant replete with stained glass, crystal and objets d'art) and the flamboyant Shuler Theatre, the construction of which caused a public outcry (whether for its Belle Epoque design or its anticipated naughty atmosphere, is difficult to deter-mine).

South of Raton, the Santa Fe Trail drove down between the long blue volcanic highlands of the Sierra Grande Arch on

From the heights of Raton Pass on the New Mexico-Colorado border, weary travelers on the Santa Fe Trail could see this heartening panorama.

THE SANTA FE TRAIL

Although Americans were not the first to attempt trade with the isolated Spanish colony of New Mexico (that honor belongs to the French, who struggled overland from Louisiana, sold their goods and were promptly booted out), they were the first to open a regular trade route—and largely through a set of fortuitous circumstances. In the summer of 1821, William Becknell, a farmer from the fledgling state of Missouri, organized an expedition to trade with the Plains Indians for horses, mules and other goods. On the plains, he chanced to meet up with a group from Santa Fe, who gave him the astonishing news of Mexican independence from Spain and invited him to enter New Mexico.

Up until this point, all trading ventures had been sharply discouraged by a Spanish government convinced (rightly, as future events would prove) that steady trade would lead to annexation; those who persevered and ventured with their pack trains into the province were unceremoniously ejected or, worse, clapped in a Chihuahua jail. But with the demise of Spanish rule, Mexican officials were inclined to view things in a different light: the people of New Mexico were

the east and the steep brown bluffs of Raton Mesa on the west. Next stop: Cimarron, headquarters of the celebrated Maxwell Land Grant and once regarded as one of the most lawless, boisterous, free-wheeling towns of the West; appropriately, "cimarron" means means "wild" or "untamed." Set against the Cimarron Range, a lovely spur of the Sangre de Cristo Mountains, the town today is a peaceful center for tourism and the logging industry; yet, just a century ago, the Las Vegas *Gazette* was reporting, "Things are quiet in Cimarron; nobody has been killed in three days."

The flamboyant town grew up around a flamboyant character: Lucien Maxwell, another of the West's multiply-occupied Renaissance men. A scout, buffalo hunter, beaver trapper and merchant, Maxwell achieved his greatest fame as owner of what was once the largest privately held parcel of land in the United States: the nearly 2-million-acre Maxwell Land Grant, a vast country of rich grazing lands and even richer gold mines. Maxwell acquired the grant through a starved for goods, and the restrictions on trade had become increasingly unpopular. So William Becknell was allowed—even invited—into New Mexico.

What he found there—the new attitude towards foreign commerce, the residents clamoring for American wares of every type—sent him hastening back to Missouri. There, to demonstrate the success of his enterprise, he allegedly spilled sacks of New Mexican silver into the stone gutters of the little town of Franklin. The clatter of that silver was heard 'round the world, and soon, a steady stream of traders was moving over the two-branched Santa Fe Trail.

Occasionally tracing over old Indian hunting paths and Spanish routes of exploration, the trail had its head in western Missouri, first at Becknell's Franklin, later at Independence or Westport. Each spring, the wagons would gather: light-weight, tough vehicles, their bodies painted light blue, their iron-rimmed wheels red, their billowing canvas covers stretched over arched hickory bows. Loaded with up to 5,000 pounds of merchandise, drawn by 10 or 12 New Mexican mules or six Missouri oxen, the wagons would strike southward, usually rendezvousing at Council Grove to organize into protective caravans.

Following the deep wheel ruts that by 1830 constituted a wide, easily followed trough—a wilderness highway—the wagon caravans crawled across the prairie. The 800-mile journey generally took about two months; whether they journeyed by way of the Mountain Branch (longer, slower, with hard pulls over the southern Rockies near Raton) or the Cimarron Cutoff (waterless, raging with hostile Indians), travelers on the trail frequently encountered hardship and danger. Rain, hail, scorching winds and clouds of dust, broken wagons and ornery mules: all were commonplaces of the trail.

They had to make it through the Jornada (a 60-mile stretch of Indian-infested, almost entirely dry barrens—also known as The Water Scrape) or up the rocky slope of Raton Pass; they had to survive colonies of rattlesnakes and alkaline streams; they even had to accustom themselves to the empty reaches that inspired such folk sayings as, "Where else can a man look so far and see so little?" But usually, in the end, it seemed worth it, for then came the triumphal entry into Santa Fe. Travelers arriving in the city at the end of the trail often were treated like heroes, crowds rushing with excited shouts of "Los Americanos!" to greet the caravans as they rumbled into the dusty Plaza.

From a commercial angle, the trip was certainly worth the trouble and risk. In 1824, just three years after Becknell's original journey, a $30,000 investment could reap $180,000: a return of 500 percent. New Mexicans loved American commercial goods: hats, gloves, ribbons, calicoes and other dry goods; building materials, tools

DENNIS & MARIA HENRY

Rabbit Ear Spring, a vital source of water for Santa Fe Trailers.

and furniture; paints, paper, ink and books; silverware and glassware; medicines and tobacco—some fast traders even sold their wagons to New Mexicans before they returned to Missouri.

Before long, American goods had enabled their purveyors to move into New Mexico and seize control of much of the region's economy. From there it was only a short step—as Spanish officials had accurately predicted—to the relatively easy annexation in 1846. The forces of General Stephen Watts Kearney came, like their commercial predecessors, over the Santa Fe Trail; they were welcomed in the capital, raising the American flag over the Plaza in bloodless triumph.

Once the Americans had control of their new Territory of New Mexico, the old Mexican tariffs, of course, were eliminated; trade over the trail increased commensurately. There were now new customers at the end of the trail, as well: prospectors drawn west by the lure of mining strikes, homesteaders looking for new lands to settle and the United States Army, whose many new forts in the area had to be plentifully supplied. This was particularly true during the Civil War years, when New Mexico served as the major far-western theater of the war; the heaviest traffic in the trail's history rumbled west between 1861 and 1865.

Ironically, these were also the last years of the trail's importance. The railroads were advancing west, pushing the eastern terminus of the trail from railhead to railhead. In 1878, the tracks of the Atchison, Topeka & Santa Fe Company were arduously laid over Raton Pass; two years later, the first engine rolled into Lamy, Santa Fe's station stop, and the Santa Fe Trail passed into legend.

DENNIS & MARIA HENRY PHOTOS

Above: The evocative adobe ruins of Fort Union, a safe harbor on the Santa Fe Trail, once the most important fort in the Southwest.
Right: Remains of Fort Union's hospital.

Facing page, top: Old Town Plaza, Las Vegas, retains its 19th-century character.
Bottom: Another view of Las Vegas Plaza, circa 1882. Most of these buildings survive intact, but today the green is canopied by shade trees.

combination of inheritance and sharp dealings, then administered it very much as a benevolent dictatorship, establishing several towns, helping numerous ranchers to get a start, and initiating an open-door policy at his enormous pile of a house, which fronted on Cimarron's town square. Gamblers, gunmen, travelers on the Santa Fe Trail: all were welcomed and lavishly entertained at Maxwell's home, which featured a gambling room, billiard parlor and dance hall.

Nobody was ever perfectly certain how big the Maxwell Land Grant really was; after Maxwell sold it to a British syndicate in 1869, the smoldering dispute over ownership of the Grant exploded into the Colfax County War. Outlaw elements—Billy the Kid, Bob Ford and Black Jack Ketchum among them—moved into Cimarron, hoping to grab a piece of the pie. Before the conflict was over, gunfights had claimed numerous victims, New Mexico's first printing press had been thrown into the Cimarron River and Cimarron had earned its deservedly bad reputation. Along with the nearly contemporaneous—and more famous—Lincoln County War, this period of frontier violence lasted several years, pointing up, once again, New Mexico's isolation; like other modern conveniences, law and order were late arrivals to the territory.

Pressing south, still along the route of the Santa Fe Trail, the eastern wave of the Sierra Grande Arch subsides, revealing at last the long burnished expanse of the Great Plains. Here the sky is a luminous bowl; in the summer, when great moist thunderclouds climb the heavens, it is possible to follow the course of a storm like the hands of a clock, swinging around the massive circle of the horizon. It is possible, also, to imagine how exposed early travelers must have felt in this enormous open landscape; there was, quite literally, nowhere to run, nowhere to hide.

What a relief it must have been, then, to glimpse, at horizon's edge, the ramparts of Fort Union; to know that safety was in reach. During a 40-year period, from 1851 to 1891, this was the largest and most important fort in the Southwest: a strategic outpost of the Civil War, the base for many of the more critical campaigns of New Mexico's Indian Wars, and the chief quartermaster depot for almost 50 forts scattered throughout the region. Perhaps most crucially, it was the primary station for troops assigned to protect travelers on the Santa Fe Trail; the Trail's two routes, the Mountain

Branch and the Cimarron Cutoff, converged some six miles south of Fort Union, after traversing the particularly dangerous, Comanche- and Kiowa-infested plains to the north and east.

It was not unknown for stagecoaches, wagons—even whole caravans—to come thundering into the fort, just ahead of a band of raiding Indians. What was truly astounding, however, was not the way the wagons arrived, but the number of them that did. In the single year of 1858, 1,827 freight wagons crossed the plains to deposit nearly 10,000 tons of merchandise in New Mexico warehouses; the volume of traffic was further enhanced by the increasing flow of settlers over the trail. And all passed by Fort Union.

With the coming of the railroad in the 1880s, the Santa Fe Trail, outmoded, withered and died; with it went the fort, which closed with the closing of the frontier. Today its adobe ruins lie scattered on the enormous prairie, looking for all the world like children's blocks, tumbled and abandoned. But what evocative ruins! The past is alive here, in the roofless officers' quarters, along the broken flagstone sidewalks, on the ghostly parade ground; to feel its power, you have only to walk in the wagon ruts that seam the short, grassy sod on the outskirts of the Fort. These are the swales of the Santa Fe Trail, scarring the prairie more than a century after the Trail languished and died; you walk in the path of hunters and traders, families and fugitives, drifters and dreamers: the Indians, Spanish and Anglos who settled our nation.

History lives on, also, in Las Vegas, some 30 miles south of Fort Union. Once the principal town on the Santa Fe Trail—renowned as the only place between Missouri and Santa Fe where a traveler could sleep in a bed—Las Vegas did not fade away along with the trail that gave it life. Instead, with the arrival of the railroad on July 4, 1879, it boomed, a "New Town," East Las Vegas, growing up alongside "Old Town." Joined by a bridge over the Gallinas River, the two Las Vegases united to become a shipping center and headquarters for the great cattle and sheep ranches of northeastern New Mexico. A brawling, lively place, the frontier city was aflame with innovation: the telephone, invented in 1876, made one of its first appearances (in 1879) in Las Vegas, which was also the first town in New Mexico to have electric light. Rolling in new wealth, the citizenry drank, gambled,

KENT KRONE

MUSEUM OF NEW MEXICO

75

RANCHING

DENNIS & MARIA HENRY

Sunrise gilds a windmill, the summit of Rabbit Ear Mountain and the grasslands of northeastern New Mexico.

Traditionally one of the mainstays of the rather limited New Mexican economy, ranching also has been the source of some of the region's bloodiest power struggles. Sheepmen versus cowmen, stockraisers versus farmers, ranchers versus oilmen, New Mexicans versus Texans: in every case, the battle has been waged over rights to some of the richest grazing lands in the world.

Long before it was cattle country, New Mexico was host to vast herds of sheep, raised first by the descendants of the Spanish who brought them to the New World, later by Indians and in recent years by newcoming Anglos. The dry New Mexican climate is perhaps even better suited to sheep than to cattle; sheep require less water, being able to absorb considerable moisture from the grass and other vegetation they ingest. Moreover, because they are smaller and need commensurately less forage, a single sheep can subsist on only 15 acres of New Mexican pastureland per year; a single cow requires about 70 acres.

Initially raised in the Rio Grande Valley and trailed to Mexico (herds totalling 250,000 were driven south in an average year), by the mid-19th century, sheep were being grazed as far east as the Llano Estacado (Staked Plains) on the Texas border, west to the San Juan Basin and north into the lush green meadows of the Colorado Rockies, then trailed by the thousands to Mexico, California and the Midwest. Sheepman Hilario Gonzales, headquartered at San Hilario on the Canadian River, was said to graze his flocks "on a thousand hills." By 1884, 5.5 million sheep were being run on New Mexican pasturelands.

Meanwhile, after the Civil War, the increasing demand for beef to feed miners, soldiers and reservation Indians led stockmen—mostly from the plains of west Texas—to begin the series of long cattle drives that play such an important role in Western legend. Texans Charles Goodnight and Oliver Loving drove their first herd of longhorns to New Mexico in the summer of 1866, entering the territory just south of present-day Carlsbad, then following the Pecos River toward the ready markets of Fort Sumner and the Bosque Redondo Reservation. The Goodnight-Loving Trail blazed the way for many others; soon New Mexico was scored with cattle thoroughfares, leading north as far as Colorado and Wyoming, and west to Arizona.

Before long, cattle not only were being driven through the state, but also were raised there in enormous numbers. By 1873, John S. Chisum, the so-called "Cow King of New Mexico" had established himself on his mammoth Jinglebob Ranch, headquartered near Roswell but running some 150 miles north to south along the Pecos River and from the Texas border on the east to Fort Sumner on the west; the Las Vegas *Gazette* described Chisum's rangelands by observing that they extended "as far as a man can travel, on a good horse, during a summer." Chisum employed a hundred hands to tend a herd numbering, at the height of his power, some 80,000 head of cattle.

Competition for holdings such as Chisum's was fierce. Cattlemen fought each other (one such battle, between Chisum and Lawrence G. Murphy, exploded into the infamous Lincoln County War), they fought sheepmen (winning a decisive victory: from the 1890s until the 1950s, the sheep industry languished), and they fought the homesteaders who moved onto their fiefdoms—basically unfenced public lands—hoping to establish farms. An interesting (if sentimental) fictional account of the struggle between cattlemen and farmers is New Mexican writer Conrad Richter's *Sea of Grass*, which mourns the passing of the open range.

Competition for land, along with the droughts and particularly hard winters of the mid-1880s, brought an end to the era of open-range cattle-raising. Today, most cattle in New Mexico are raised scientifically, on fenced ranges, by large-scale ranchers or corporations. The industry is still vital—the sale of beef now accounts for more than half of all New Mexico's receipts from agricultural products—but romance has gone down the trail with the Goodnights, the Lovings and the Chisums.

shopped for suddenly available consumer goods and engaged in a flurry of building, producing elegant hotels, bustling mercantiles, huge warehouses and dazzling new homes, all in an exuberant array of late-Victorian architectural styles: Greek Revival and Queen Anne to Romanesque and Italianate.

The pace has slowed today, the decline of the railroad draining away much of Las Vegas's youthful vigor, but the town is still an architectural treasure trove, its ornate Victorians sitting cheek-by-jowl with even more venerable adobes in several historic districts. The Plaza District, in particular, is a monument to the glitter of Victorian commerce, its ornate facades laid out around the tree-shaded square where a windmill once stood, its sails utilized for the occasional spontaneous hanging. The square is dominated—as it has been since 1881—by the massively grand Plaza Hotel, now meticulously renovated and welcoming guests once more. Here, too, tucked beneath the crenelated parapets of a former law office, is a wonderful bookstore, Los Artesanos, specializing in Western—and particularly New Mexican—literature, arts and history.

From Las Vegas, travelers on the Santa Fe Trail had to make one final push before reaching their goal: between the high hogback ridges of the Glorieta Pass, its ledges and slopes formed by the gradual erosion of sandstone, mudstone and siltstone deposited in eons past by a warm, shallow sea. Against the rock escarpment, they could see—as we can today—the ruins of Pecos Pueblo.

When Coronado first arrived in New Mexico, this was the region's largest Indian city, its two great four-story communal dwellings containing more than a thousand rooms clustered about five plazas and served by 16 ceremonial kivas. Under Spanish supervision, a reputedly beautiful mission church, Nuestra Senora de los Angeles de Porciuncula, was built here in 1617; hewn from the local reddish stone, its windows were fitted with thin layers of nearly transparent gypsum. After it was burned in the Pueblo Revolt, another church of adobe was constructed within its foundations, but by the 1830s, Pecos's population had been so decimated by disease, depredation and Apache attacks that the pueblo was abandoned, and swiftly fell to ruins. These remnants are preserved today as the Pecos National Monument.

Glorieta Pass is renowned not only as the last leg of the

A restored kiva at Pecos National Monument. STEPHEN TRIMBLE

Santa Fe Trail; it was also the site of a decisive Civil War engagement, the Battle of Glorieta Pass, often referred to as "the Gettysburg of the West." Led by Major John M. Chivington and his First Colorado Volunteers, this bloody series of struggles on March 26 and 28, 1862 led to the destruction of a Confederate supply depot and forced a Rebel retreat back to Fort Bliss, Texas, thus ending the Confederacy's hopes for a western empire. As one Texan soldier wrote to his wife, "If it had not been for those devils from Pike's Peak, this country would have been ours."

Immediately after the Civil War, most travelers coming through Glorieta Pass had been forced to make their way west over the Mountain Branch of the Santa Fe Trail; the Cimarron Cutoff had become, with the post-war increase in Indian-American hostilities, a suicide run. Plains Indians (primarily Comanche, Apache, Kiowa and Arapaho) roamed the Cutoff

Above: The sea of grass, Kiowa National Grasslands.

Facing page, left: Lichen-encrusted volcanic rock, Capulin Mountain National Monument.
Top: Volcanic cones viewed from the top of Capulin Volcano, Capulin Mountain National Monument.
Bottom: Wagon Mound, created by several flows of molten lava, one of the most important landmarks on the Santa Fe Trail.

prairie shimmered, alive and waving with each passing breeze. But the sea of grass is no more; ranching, the life's blood of the region, has laid it waste with grazing—and overgrazing.

The whole eastern portion of the state, north and south—known collectively as the East Side—has provided rich fodder for stockmen raising both sheep and cattle. Suffering from the drought that is a persistent obstacle in the Southwest, and from territorial battles first with homesteading farmers and later with wildcatters looking for oil and petroleum, ranching nevertheless has remained an economic keystone of the area, and of New Mexico in general (see page 76: Ranching).

The prairies as they were before the advent of large-scale ranching—tall, wide and open—may be glimpsed at the Kiowa National Grasslands, a 136,000-acre preserve east of Clayton. The U.S. Forest Service administers the grasslands, paradoxically conducting studies there with the University of New Mexico in the health, nutrition and management of cattle. Nearby, too, is Clayton Lake State Park, where it is possible to see the crater-like footprints of creatures who roamed the northeastern range long before cattle—or man—existed; hundreds of dinosaur tracks are preserved there in a two-acre stretch of Cretaceous sandstone.

Many of the major landmarks on the Santa Fe Trail's Cimarron Cutoff are monuments also to the volcanic activity that raged in this region's distant past. Rabbit Ear Mountain (a distinctly un-rabbitlike formation named for an Indian chief) is a gently eroded volcano terraced with lava; Wagon Mound, to the south, was created by two lava flows (and it does, indeed, resemble the billowing canvas of a covered wagon!). But perhaps the most notable remnant of the area's violent volcanism is Capulin Mountain, the centerpiece of 775-acre Capulin Mountain National Monument.

Rising 1,500 feet above its surrounding plain, Capulin is what geologists call a "classic" cinder cone, formed less than 10,000 years ago when ash and cinders piled up around a vent from which they had abruptly exploded. Lava flowed from a vent at the volcano's base, which accounts for its almost perfectly preserved cone shape, gouged with a 415-foot-deep crater. The cone is highest on its northeast side because winds at the time of Capulin's eruption blew ash in that direction; prevailing winds in the area still blow from the southwest.

It is distinctly possible that the eruption of Capulin was

from Kansas through the Oklahoma Panhandle and into New Mexico, running off stock, burning wagons, taking captives, killing, scalping and mutilating their victims—treating them, in fact, much as the United States Army and various vigilante groups treated Indians during the many notorious massacres that blacken this period in our history.

The dauntless souls who, determined to make fast work of the Santa Fe Trail, still traveled by the Cimarron Cutoff entered New Mexico far to the northeast, at McNees Crossing, a few miles north of present-day Clayton. The landscape here is vast and lonely, its gently rolling plains punctuated by eroded volcanoes, the outlying remnants of a volcanic field centered at nearby Capulin National Monument. This portion of the Great Plains is underlain by the gravel and sand of the Ogallala Formation, a porous combination that quickly absorbs rainfall and snowmelt, thus slowing erosion; here, as on the plains surrounding Fort Union, massive swales of the Santa Fe Trail are still visible. In fact, little in this landscape has changed in the last century, with one important exception: a hundred years ago, the grass grew saddle high and the whole

KENT & DONNA DANNEN

DENNIS & MARIA HENRY

DENNIS & MARIA HENRY

viewed by Folsom Man, the prehistoric hunter named for the nearby hamlet of Folsom, where his finely shaped flint spear points were discovered early in this century by cowboy George McJunkin. Folsom Man was, after all, firmly established in the region 10,000 years ago; geologist Halka Chronic reports that charcoal from this prehistoric New Mexican's fires has been used (via carbon-14 dating techniques) to help pinpoint the age of Capulin's ashy remnants.

Prehistoric man and the Santa Fe Trail, Indian wars and carbon dating: once again, in the northeast, the familiar New Mexico alchemy is at work. Oddly, for all its diverse and rather haunting charms, this is one of the less-visited corners of the state. Perhaps its topography—the vast, exposed reaches, the looming volcanic shapes—seems intimidating. Yet it is a landscape whose beauty deepens with acquaintance, offering a broad perspective—on time, on history—to match its wide-open spaces.

SOUTHEAST

STAKED PLAINS AND SPACE SHOTS

KENT & DONNA DANNEN

Above: *A brilliant day's end over El Capitan Mountain west of Roswell.*

Facing page: *Sunset paints the dunes purple, White Sands National Monument.*

From a geologist's point of view, southeastern New Mexico offers a true embarrassment of riches. Enough geological wonders are gathered here—the gleaming gypsum dunes of White Sands, the ropy black basalt lava flows of the Valley of Fires, the seemingly endless expanse of the Llano Estacado, the stunningly shaped and colored limestone of Carlsbad Caverns—to make even a jaded expert feel alternately dazzled and overwhelmed.

The history buff, too, must experience the mixed emotions of excitement and overload when confronted by the richness of this region. Here, the spear points of prehistoric Clovis Man lie within a few miles of Trinity Site, where the first atomic bomb was exploded in 1945. Lincoln, the haunt of notorious outlaw Billy the Kid, lies just up a mountain road from Roswell, where Dr. Robert Goddard designed and built liquid-fuel rockets. And on the Llano Estacado, cattle run where they have for over a century—often grazing around humming machinery extracting gas and oil from beneath the doubly rich grasslands.

The Llano Estacado—the Staked Plains—is bedded on sedimentary rock capped with a huge layer of gravel and sand, stream-carried debris of the Southern Rockies. This layer—the Ogallala Formation—once extended west all the way to the foothills of the Sangre de Cristos; over time, much of it has been worn away. But in patches of northeastern New Mexico, in much of the state's southeastern quadrant and on into West Texas, the Llano Estacado has remained virtually unchanged for millions of years. Here, its caprock is impregnated with caliche, a hard, crusty, porous white rock that absorbs water readily, so preventing the development of eroding streams; this effect has been enhanced by the area's erosion-resistant vegetation: the thick, tough sod of buffalo grass.

Named by Spanish soldiers who likened its surrounding rock escarpments to military barricades built from long stakes, the 20,000-square-mile tableland of the Llano Estacado is flat, featureless, often desolate. Rain falling on the Llano runs nowhere; it is either evaporated by the region's harsh winds (whose average velocity, unchecked by tree or mountain, is the highest in the nation) or it percolates into the ground. Occasionally, unpredictably, this balm of the plains will then seep forth, forming shallow, ephemeral, often bitter-watered lakes, their surfaces rippled, in the winter months, by the fawn-colored wings of migrating lesser sandhill cranes. One such place, managed as a preserve for the cranes and other waterfowl, is Bitter Lake Wildlife Refuge, near Roswell.

Ranchers and farmers have learned to drive their wells deep to tap the Llano Estacado's reserves of sustaining water, but until technology caught up with desire, the Llano was a forbidding place, a dry and hazardous barrier reinforcing New Mexico's isolation. There were, however, a few intrepid souls who dared to venture onto its sere reaches: the Comanche, trailing herds of buffalo, and a motley group of traders looking to do business with them: the infamous Comancheros.

Wily, durable and indisputably profit-minded, the Comancheros were primarily Hispanics, Pueblo Indians and genizaros who at first confined their commerce to trinkets, hides and food-stuffs; soon, however, they had branched out, illegally trading guns, ammunition and whiskey for the literally hundreds of thousands of cattle rustled by the Comanche from the ranches of New Mexico and Texas. Because their trading grounds were in the remote canyons fringing the Llano, the Comancheros remained for many years virtually untouchable.

Nature trail through the twisted black lava flows of Valley of Fires State Park.

economy." This laissez-faire attitude about stock primarily Texan in origin did little to improve relations between New Mexico and the Lone Star State, long-time enemies. Texans saw themselves as victims, while New Mexicans pointed out that the Texans were the original raiders, having twice tried to grab huge portions of southeast New Mexico, up to and including the Rio Grande.

Today, the Texans have, in some sense, got their own back. With the opening of the Llano Estacado first as valuable cattle range and later as the source of rich oil and natural gas preserves, thousands of Texans have flooded into southeastern New Mexico. With Texan immigrants exerting considerable influence over such ranching and energy-boom towns as Clovis, Portales, Hobbs and Artesia, the region is often referred to as "Little Texas." Texans—and Texan money—have also been instrumental in the development of a local resort, Ruidoso, on the eastern slope of the Sacramento Mountains; there, each year, the world's biggest, richest quarterhorse races are run, one with a purse of more than $2 million. "Biggest," "richest": there are those who feel that these appellations ring with a decidedly Texan twang not particularly appropriate in New Mexico.

Ruidoso, nevertheless, has its charms, chief among them its setting amidst the pine-clad peaks of the Sacramento Mountains. Precambrian granite capped with beautifully swirled strata of sedimentary rock, the Sacramentos reveal their geological history most clearly in the lovely striped layers visible where the mountains' western flanks tower over the Tularosa Basin near Alamogordo. At twilight, these high, stepped bluffs glow rose and violet, rising stiffly over the basin floor like the walls of some splendidly fortified dream city.

To the east, rock walls give way to high mountain meadows and lush valleys, the ancient homeland of the Mescalero Apache. Guarded by the soaring volcanic peak of their sacred mountain, Sierra Blanca, their 460,000-acre reservation is enriched by stands of timber and grassy ranchlands which handily support the tribe, as do the throngs of tourists who flock to enjoy the area's stunning scenery and wide array of recreational opportunities. Surprisingly, the Mescalero—one of the last tribes to submit to Anglo authority—have come up with some decidedly Anglo-oriented business enterprises designed to lure these tourists and their dollars: the Indian-

There was, furthermore, a very good reason for allowing their business to go on unmolested: the Comancheros also traded in captives, ransoming them from the Indians not out of altruism, but for the profit they might turn by selling these unfortunates back to their desperate families. Often, the Comancheros provided the only hope for such families, whose loved ones had frequently been snatched from as far away as Mexico or Colorado; officials could only shudder, imagining the public outcry if that last hope was taken away. So the government compromised, inaugurating a series of virtually unenforceable regulations, but allowing the Comancheros to continue their admittedly dirty dealings. A blood-curdling portrait of Comanchero ruthlessness, incidentally, is the character of Blue Duck in Larry McMurtry's wonderful novel, *Lonesome Dove.*

With all the to-do surrounding the introduction of new laws designed to control Comanchero trading, little was said about the enormous numbers of rustled cattle passing through their hands; perhaps, as historian David Lavender suggests, "because of the stolen animals' importance to New Mexico's

THE APACHE

Once the most feared warriors and raiders of the Southwest, the Apache—a loosely organized group of tribal bands—began their life in the region as relatively peaceful, nomadic hunter-gatherers. From their point of origin somewhere to the north, they wandered through New Mexico, the Jicarilla (named after their finely woven baskets, or jicarillas) settling in the north, in the rolling high country west of the Rio Grande; the Mescalero (so-called because of their taste for the mescal plant) fanning out into the southeast's Sacramento Mountains; the Chiricahua scattering to the deserts and canyons of southwestern New Mexico and eastern Arizona. There, living in tipis or wickiups, they followed the buffalo and developed cordial relations with neighboring Pueblo Indians, trading and picking up the rudiments of agriculture.

But with first Spanish, then Anglo encroachment on their lands and against the herds of buffalo that were their life's blood, the Apache were forced to take up arms, conducting some of the fiercest wars fought on the frontier. Hopelessly outnumbered, they continued their fight until 1886, longer than virtually any other Native American tribe, led by some of the most perspicacious minds in strategic

history: Geronimo, Victorio and Nana (who was 70 years old when he began his part in the Indian wars).

The Mescalero and Jicarilla Apache were granted reservations in areas corresponding, more or less, with their original homelands; the Chiricahua were not so fortunate. Because they had been at war with the United States longer and more persistently than any other Apache group, they were exiled to Florida; in 1913, they were finally given permission to return to New Mexico to live with the Mescalero.

Because of their nomadic heritage, the Apache developed few of the crafts traditions that have sustained their Pueblo neighbors; basketmaking, however, has lately seen something of a revival among, appropriately enough, the Jicarilla. Until recently, both Jicarilla and Mescalero have depended on the old pursuits of stockraising and farming to support their tribes. In their struggle to become economically self-sufficient, however, the Apache have lately taken advantage of such contemporary phenomena as the discovery of oil on the Jicarilla reservation and the possibilities for tourism in the Mescalero's scenic section of the Sacramento Mountains. The Mescalero, moreover, hold a federal charter, which has given them the right to borrow large sums of money from the federal government for the development of their various enterprises. This they have done with, it must be admitted, varying degrees of success.

MUSEUM OF NEW MEXICO

But if Apache tribal life has changed in many ways, certain rites and rituals remain as potent as in the days of old. Chief among these is the Apache Puberty Ceremony, portions of which may be witnessed by non-Indians. A coming-of-age ritual for Apache girls, the four-day ceremony is designed to confer upon them the four qualities of the sacred White Painted Lady: strength, patience, good luck and wisdom. At the Mescalero ceremonial, much of the rite is still performed by the awesomely garbed and painted Mountain Spirit Dancers, or *gans*. Among the Jicarilla, the dancers have not been used since tribal officials decreed that no one who had been vaccinated could be a Mountain Spirit dancer; the result was the disqualification of virtually all Jicarilla youth.

Mescalero Apache at Santa Fe's Tertio-Millenial Exposition, 1883. At this time, several Apache groups still were waging their hopeless but noble battle to retain their homelands.

Perhaps as compensation, the Jicarilla have another ritual, a gathering held annually at their reservation's Stone Lake. Like the nomads they once were, the Jicarilla come to camp out on the grassy slopes surrounding the lake, each family building a brush shelter or raising a tipi. As the night deepens, fires flare along the hillsides, and drums sound out, echoing deep and resonant over the still lake waters. It is a scene from another time, when the Apache roamed a land they could truly call their own.

DENNIS & MARIA HENRY PHOTOS

Above: Tunstall Store Museum, Lincoln, with original merchandise. This mercantile operation was the focus of much of the Lincoln County War.

Right: The Torreon, a masonry fortification built in Lincoln in the 1850s to protect settlers from Indian attacks.

Facing page: The limestone formations of the Temple of the Sun, Carlsbad Caverns.

owned and -operated Sierra Blanca ski resort and the ultra-luxurious year-round resort, the Inn of the Mountain Gods (see page 83: The Apache).

Northeast of the Mescalero Reservation, tucked into a pastoral fold of the surrounding hills, is a tiny country hamlet first settled by the Spaniards in the 1850s. They called it La Placita del Rio Bonito (The Little Town by the Pretty River); ironically, this serene spot, renamed Lincoln, became the locus of one of the bloodiest power struggles of the old Southwest, the Lincoln County War.

Beginning in 1878, this ugly struggle over who would control the region's economy in general—and lucrative government beef contracts in particular—turned Lincoln into a shooting gallery, launched William Bonney, better known as Billy the Kid, on his life of crime, and culminated in a three-day gun battle, by the end of which most of the principals in the conflict were dead. But the violence was not over; in 1881, Billy the Kid, after a long spree of rustling and killing, was captured, convicted and brought back to Lincoln to be hanged. In perhaps the most dramatic episode of his ill-starred career, he killed the men who were guarding him at the Lincoln County courthouse and made a stunning escape. A few months later, Sheriff Pat Garrett caught up with the Kid at Fort Sumner; two bullets wrote an end to the outlaw's story (see page 86: The Lincoln County War).

Today Lincoln, although considerably quieter, looks virtually as it did in its days of lawlessness. Its pretty adobe houses, the two stores that were focal points of the War, the courthouse and the Wortley Hotel—still an operating inn and restaurant—have all been preserved as an historic district, a state monument administered by the Museum of New Mexico. Every August, local residents stage a hilarious reenactment of Billy the Kid's brazen escape from the Courthouse; this is accompanied by such events as a fiddlers' contest and a Pony Express race from the ghost town of White Oaks to Lincoln, the riders carrying mail that has been specially cancelled for philatelists who go in for that sort of thing. Such are the uses of history.

History of a very different kind was made to the east, near the confluence of the Pecos River and the Rio Hondo. There, in the 1870s, New Mexican Cow King John Chisum (one of the few participants in the Lincoln County War to survive and prosper) established his own personal fiefdom, the Jinglebob Ranch, thus catalyzing the development of the town of Roswell. The little town's good luck continued with the 1891 discovery that it was lying on top of a vast artesian basin fed by precipitation seeping into the Permian limestone slopes of the eastern Sacramentos. Water running down these slopes builds up what geologists call hydrostatic "head," which means that it bubbles to the surface in springs or rises in wells without being pumped. Armed with new, seemingly inexhaustible supplies of water, Roswell—along with such nearby communities as Hobbs and the aptly named Artesia—found agriculture joining ranching as the backbone of its burgeoning economy.

But it was still another discovery that transformed Roswell from a prosperous community into a boom town. The porous limestone basin underlying the town was, it turned out, not a reservoir just for water, but also for rich reserves of oil and gas, produced by the slow decomposition of plant and animal material within the Permian rock. As these resources began to be tapped in the 1920s and 1930s, Roswell (along with Artesia and Hobbs) saw much of its range and farmland turned into oil fields strewn with rocking pumps or gas fields spangled with the twisting pipes of gas line "Christmas trees." A faint odor of gas drifts across these still-active fields.

The limestone that has contributed so powerfully to the prosperity of much of southeastern New Mexico also has provided one of the region's most fascinating geological wonders, and one of the state's most popular tourist attractions: the spectacular Carlsbad Caverns. Formed from a massive reef laid down in Permian time (290 to 240 million years ago) in a lagoon at the edge of an inland sea, the caverns developed over millions of years as their porous limestone was dissolved and channeled by the flow of mineral-rich water. Once the water table dropped in the enlarged channelways— the caverns themselves—leaving them dry, the continuing seepage of water from their ceilings, down their walls and over their surfaces created the eerily beautiful stalactites and stalagmites, the delicate draperies and scalloped travertine deposits we may view today.

While southwestern New Mexico is notable for the manifold riches of its ranchlands, artesian water supplies and precious natural resources, it was something else entirely that

TOM TILL

JACK OLSON

Above: The International Space Hall of Fame, Alamogordo.

made it the site of choice for the experiments of physicist-inventor Dr. Robert H. Goddard. Goddard had begun his work in the development of liquid-fuel rockets near the small town of Auburn, Massachusetts; there, however, tumultuously loud and occasionally aborted test flights began to alarm local officials. Looking for some wide open spaces in which to conduct further tests, Goddard hit on the region around Roswell, which became his headquarters.

There, on the lonely, rolling prairies, he became the first to shoot a liquid-fuel rocket faster than the speed of sound. He obtained the first patents for a rocket steering apparatus and for the use of "step rockets" to reach higher altitudes. He developed the first rocket fuel pumps and self-cooling rocket motors. His tiny rockets, early prototypes of the modern moon thrusters, eventually achieved altitudes of more than a mile above the plains.

And yet, despite these remarkable achievements, despite
(continued on page 89)

The origins of the Lincoln County War—surely one of the most violent episodes in the history of New Mexico's, and America's, very violent frontier—are so complex that they have engendered numerous conflicting accounts: from the lurid newspaper report written on the spot to the learned historical treatise penned—or computered—only yesterday. From this mountain of data, one unshakeable fact emerges: no one in the conflict was operating from a high moral ground. The Lincoln County War was a power struggle, hardly pure but certainly simple, over who would control the economic and political life of Lincoln County and of much of New Mexico, as well.

Lining up on one side of the conflict were local merchant king L.G. Murphy; his associate, James J. Dolan; and Santa Fe robber baron-politician Thomas Catron. On the other were John H. Tunstall, an English rancher and merchant; the Scottish attorney and deal-maker Alexander McSween; and powerful cattleman John Chisum. Until the late 1870s, Murphy's mercantile firm, L.G. Murphy and Company (commonly known as "The House"), held a virtual stranglehold on the life of Lincoln County. Aided and abetted by the political machinations of Catron (a member of the notoriously corrupt Santa Fe Ring), Murphy and his cohorts bought goods cheaply, then sold them at inflated prices; extended credit freely, then foreclosed mercilessly; seized the real estate of those they had ruined and then, although title was often in doubt, sold or leased these lands to newcomers who had no idea what they were getting into. Their economic and, consequently, political power was absolute; at one point, Murphy strode imperiously into a nominating convention that was not going his way, overturned tables and tossed papers into the air, then informed the stunned audience that "You might as well try to stop the waves of the ocean with a fork as to try and oppose me."

This is exactly what the Tunstall-McSween-Chisum faction attempted to do, competing for the lucrative government beef contracts that were part of the The House's stock in trade, initiating a series of lawsuits designed to break the monopoly's hold on Lincoln County, and even opening their own store just down the Lincoln street from Murphy's. With pressures mounting, the conflict exploded into violence on February 18, 1878, when a posse instigated by the Murphy-Dolan group ambushed and murdered John Tunstall.

Among Tunstall's ranch hands was a young man, William Bonney, who went by the name of Billy the Kid. Until then, Billy had been "an amiable lad whose brushes with the law had not been unduly serious by southwestern standards" (this characterization from David Lavender, whose

excellent history, *The Southwest*, contains one of the more lucid and compelling treatments of the Lincoln County War). Realizing, however, that his employer's death stood little chance of being legally avenged in Murphy/Dolan-dominated Lincoln County, Billy took the law into his own hands, organizing a vigilante group, The Regulators. Within a few months, retributive killings were the order of the day, and the peaceful town of Lincoln had turned into an armed camp.

The climax came in July, when the two warring factions engaged in a three-day gun battle up and down the Lincoln street, ending with the torching of McSween's home and the killing of five men, including McSween himself. Billy the Kid—on this, as on other occasions—managed to make his escape. President Rutherford B. Hayes, alarmed by the magnitude of Lincoln's lawlessness, intervened at this point, dismissing the Catron-coopted territorial Governor of New Mexico, Samuel Axtell, and appointing Civil War General Lew Wallace with a stern directive to clean up the mess in Lincoln County.

This Wallace accomplished (also managing to finish his novel, *Ben Hur,* during off moments at the Governor's Palace), first by offering a blanket amnesty to those who would testify about the events in Lincoln, then (after yet another McSween associate, Huston Chapman, was gunned down in full view of such witnesses as Billy the Kid) by visiting Lincoln for six weeks

DENNIS & MARIA HENRY

to investigate the situation personally. At one point, he even had a secret meeting with Billy the Kid, hoping to persuade him to testify about the Chapman murder. This hope was dashed when the men arrested for the killing broke out of jail and vanished.

No one, it seems, had to endure much in the way of punishment for taking part in the Lincoln County War. Some lit out from the law, others plea-bargained and were found guilty of lesser charges. James Dolan had his indictment quashed; Thomas Catron continued his double dealings as a member in good standing of the Santa Fe Ring; former Governor Axtell even went on to be appointed Chief Justice of the New Mexico Supreme Court. Only L.G. Murphy suffered, dying—just a few months after the murder of his old enemy McSween—of drink.

Billy the Kid, meanwhile, moved on to a life of crime in earnest, rustling and killing until his arrest in San Miguel County some months later. Tried for

The Lincoln County Courthouse, from which Billy the Kid made his violent escape. Legend has it that the Kid, before he fled, danced with glee on the courthouse balcony.

murder, he was sentenced to be hanged in Lincoln on Friday the 13th of May, 1881. But before the hangman could get his noose around Billy's young throat, the outlaw engineered a daring daylight escape from the jail at the Lincoln County Courthouse, shooting one of his guards, J.W. Bell, with Bell's own pistol, then grabbing a shotgun and killing another guard, Robert Ollinger, who was running across the street to see what all the shooting was about. Billy remained at large for less than three months; on the evening of July 13 (some say 14), 1881, Pat Garrett (elected sheriff of Lincoln County on a strict law-and-order ticket) found him in the back bedroom of a ranch at Fort Sumner and ended his life with two swift shots in the dark.

the continuing support—both financial and moral—of such advocates as aviation pioneer Charles Lindbergh and industrialist-philanthropist Harry F. Guggenheim, Goddard was rarely taken seriously. The press, in fact, labeled him "Moony" Goddard, and his hopes for travel beyond the earth were a source of considerable public amusement.

At the beginning of World War II, Goddard offered his work to the U.S. military. Unable to envision a use for rocketry, they turned him down. But the Germans read his research reports, and used them to develop their own rockets, including the V-2 that wrought havoc on London in 1944. When Germany's top rocket scientist, Werner von Braun, was captured by Americans after the war, he was asked how the V-2 worked. His succinct reply: "Why don't you ask Goddard?" By this time, however, just at the threshold of the rocket age, Goddard was dead. Posthumously, he was awarded the Congressional Gold Medal, and a million-dollar settlement was made for the use of his patents. His name is honored today at the Goddard Space Center.

Southeastern New Mexico's ideal suitability for aviation and, more recently, aerospace testing has made it a continuing leader in rocket and allied research. Across the Sacramentos from Roswell, near the booming Tularosa Basin town of Alamogordo, are Holloman Air Force Base—with its Air Force Missile Development Center—and the White Sands Missile Range. Closely allied with these centers is the Sacramento Peak Observatory, located just a few miles from a lovely mountain resort with the appropriately romantic and lofty name of Cloudcroft.

In a remote part of the White Sands Missile Range is Trinity Site, the fateful spot where another kind of experimentation bore its dread fruit on July 16, 1945 with the explosion of the world's first atomic bomb. Trinity may be visited, but on only two days a year, one in April, the other in October.

More easily—and happily—approached is White Sands National Monument, a short drive west of Alamogordo. A gleaming 146,535-acre expanse of snow-white dunes formed (unlike most dunes, which are composed of silica or quartz sand) from disintegrated gypsum crystals, the monument is one of the more uniquely beautiful of all New Mexico's many attractions. The original source of the White Sands dunes—some rising 60 feet above the floor of the Tularosa Basin—are

Above: Tenacious cottonwoods cling to the shifting sands, White Sands National Monument.
Left: Strawberry cactus at White Sands.

Facing page: Rainstorm over White Sands National Monument.

89

STEPHEN TRIMBLE

GLENN VAN NIMWEGEN

Above: Sierra Blanca, sacred to the Mescalero Apache, seen from the Indian-administered resort, the Inn of the Mountain Gods.
Right: A collared lizard perches on volcanic rock, Valley of Fires State Park.

Facing page, top left: Protective coloration: a lizard has taken on the hue of its surroundings at White Sands National Monument.
Top right: Old railroad trestle near the Sacramento Mountain town of Cloudcroft.
Bottom: Street scene during the 1920s in the oil-boom town of Hobbs.

gypsum deposits left in the sediment-striped rock of the nearby San Andres Mountains some 250 million years ago. Rainwater and snowmelt convey large quantities of this gypsum to Lake Lucero in the southwestern portion of the monument; there, the region's hot, dry winds evaporate the lake and its surrounding alkali flats and the crystalline gypsum (selenite) is gradually broken into fine particles. These ride the winds to the northeast, where they are piled into glowing, endlessly shifting dunes. This entire process of dune-building has taken place in a relatively short span of time; in geological terms, White Sands is virtually newborn—just 25,000 years old.

No two visits to the monument can ever be the same, for the face of the dunefield is in a state of constant flux. Sand-storms—common in the area during February, March and April—blow up to 45 miles per hour, moving countless tons of sand within periods of a few hours. Much of the monument's sparse vegetation has a tenuous hold on life, not, surprisingly, because of lack of moisture (while the air at White Sands is extremely dry, plentiful water lies beneath the sands, quite close to the surface), but rather because of the constant movement of their growth medium. Amazingly, plants such as the soaptree yucca and the skunkbush sumac, the rubber rabbitbrush and the Rio Grande cottonwood have developed some extraordinary adaptive techniques for staying on top of the onrushing dunes, from elongating their stems to growing root systems that actually stabilize sand.

Wildlife, too, has had to adapt to live among the dunes. The western hognose snake has learned to dig down below the sandy surface to get at the moisture it requires; several species of toads have developed compressed life cycles, confined to the area's brief rainy season. Perhaps most astonishing is the broad range of animals—from mice to lizards to crickets—that have protectively adapted their coloration to their environment—and turned white. This becomes even more amazing when one realizes that just 30 miles north of White Sands, amidst the knotted ebony lava flows of the Valley of Fires State Park, live many similar animals; similar, that is, except for one particular: they are black.

There are any number of "classic" ways to view White Sands: in the full flood of day, sunlight lending additional brilliance to the luster of the fine white gypsum hills; at sunset,

GLENN VAN MINWEGEN

ROBERT M. COTTEN

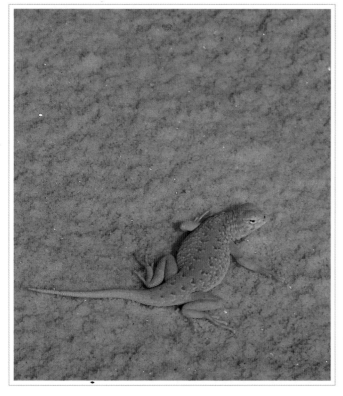

when the shadows are long and the dunes tinged pink; at night, with the moon shedding its silver over the answering, unearthly landscape. I have even visited the dunes after a spring storm, finding their silky surface pocked and channeled by rain, their distant rim of mountains capped with towering blue thunderclouds lending, by contrast, an almost preternatural intensity to that whole luminous world of white.

It is hardly surprising to learn that such a landscape has yielded a rich and varied trove of artifacts. Deep in the monument's interior dunes, patrolling park rangers have uncovered prehistoric spear points, Mescalero grinding stones, weathered remains of 18th-century Spanish salt carts, spent cavalry cartridges and even fragments of lost missiles: the history of White Sands, of the southeast, of New Mexico, all revealed by the sudden shift of these moving sands.

MUSEUM OF NEW MEXICO

SOUTHWEST

CHAPTER SEVEN

ROCK OF AGES

DENNIS & MARIA HENRY

Above: *Sunset lends an aura of mystery to the eroded volcanic forms at City of Rocks State Park.*

Facing page: *Wintering sandhill cranes are shadowed by a flight of snow geese at the Bosque del Apache Wildlife Refuge.*

The story of southwestern New Mexico is written in its rock: the volcanic rock that forms much of the region's jumbled geology, the rock cliffs that sheltered the people of the ancient Mogollon Culture, the ore-rich rock whose veins of gold, silver and copper have lured treasure-seekers to the area in a recurring cycle of booms and busts that continues to the present day.

A large portion of the region is given over to the Datil-Mogollon Highlands, a volcanic field layered with lava and ash; marked by vast, deeply eroded calderas; and slashed by fault-edged sunken blocks, among them the broad expanse of the Plains of San Agustin. Occupying a beautiful, flat-floored valley ringed with misty blue mountains, these plains once were washed by a Pleistocene lake some 50 miles long; today, they are the site of the National Radio Astronomy Observatory's Very Large Array: a group of 27 huge, saucer-shaped antennae distributed along railroad tracks arranged in a gigantic Y.

These antennae gather radio signals from interstellar space, many of them emitted millions, even billions of years ago, and only now reaching earth. Such signals help scientists to study phenomena including the birth and death of stars and the properties of galaxies similar to our own; at some point, enough data may be gathered to put together a clear picture of the origins of our universe. Even if one knows absolutely nothing about radioastronomy, the antennae of the Very Large Array are a sight to behold, their enormous white saucers turned beseechingly to the heavens, as if awaiting the answer to some very important question. Which, of course, they are.

Just east of the Plains of San Agustin lie the Magdalena Mountains, a small volcanic range seamed with lead-silver

ores left behind when their Paleozoic limestone was altered by the intrusion of molten rock bearing the precious metals in fluid form. Beginning in the 1860s, and reaching a peak in the 1880s, such whimsically-named but fortune-producing mines as the Graphic, the Hardscrabble, the Vindicator and the Ambrosia shipped millions of dollars worth of lead-silver ore from the so-called Magdalena District; a single town in the district, Kelly, produced $28.4 million worth of lead, zinc, silver, copper and a small amount of gold before being abandoned in 1945.

The development of the Magdalena District had far-reaching effects, nowhere more profoundly felt than in the little hamlet of Socorro. Located on the eastern side of the Magdalenas, the town was allegedly named by a group of Spaniards for the aid (succor) extended to them by friendly local Indians when they stumbled in, parched and starving, from the dread badlands of the Jornada del Muerto. Long a sleepy Hispanic farming settlement, Socorro was transformed by the Magdalena strikes into a raucous mining town.

At the height of the madness, 44 saloons provided round-the-clock entertainment and libation, engendering some of the wilder episodes in the history of the southwestern frontier. Perhaps best remembered is the legend of Deputy Sheriff Elfego Baca who, over the course of a 36-hour gunfight, managed to hold off some 80 Texans enraged because he'd had the temerity to arrest one of their inebriated compatriots. The heroic Baca went on to become, among other things, an assistant district attorney and the mayor of Socorro. And although the silver boom eventually went bust, Socorro remains a mining center of sorts as the home of the New Mexico Institute of Mining and Technology.

Southeast of Socorro, near the farming center of San

92

DAN PEHA

Above: Elephant Butte is reflected in the reservoir that bears its name, near Truth or Consequences.

Facing page: The deeply eroded crags of the Organ Mountains jut over southwestern New Mexico's largest city, Las Cruces.

fire, wave after wave coming in to settle down for the night, the air ringing with their constant honks and cries. One is reminded of what these lands must have been—teeming with life—before the encroachment of human settlement here.

Man's persistent push into untrammeled lands is, of course, an inevitability, and not always one that leads into paradisiacal regions flowing with milk and honey. This the Spanish found out as they moved into New Mexico over the broad, withered plain that came to be known as the Jornada del Muerto, the Journey of Death. Ninety miles long, 35 miles wide, the Jornada runs roughly south from the Bosque del Apache to present-day Rincon, flanked on either side by the tilted, sediment-striped ranges of the Rio Grande Rift.

At one time, millions of years ago, the Rio Grande flowed through the Jornada. As fault movement deepened its present course, however, the river abandoned the plain, leaving it a closed valley, notable primarily for its utter lack of water. Despite this, the Jornada became a frequently used branch of El Camino Real, the Royal Road north from New Spain, because it offered a swift route often—though not always—safer from Indian attack than the almost parallel way up the Rio Grande Valley.

Stories of the early Spanish parties who perished from thirst while trying to cross the Jornada are legion; one group was saved only because they were travelling with a little dog who managed to sniff out a spring hidden in a bordering canyon. A fitting coda to the history of the Jornada was written in 1945 when the first atomic bomb was detonated at Trinity Site, at the southeastern tip of the Journey of Death.

West of the Jornada, the Rio Grande meanders through its valley, lapped on either side by terraces and alluvial fans. On the river's eastern bank, near the glassy green surface of the Elephant Butte Reservoir (named for the elephant-shaped volcanic neck jutting up beside it), thermal springs bubble to the surface, their 110-degree waters valued for hundreds of years for their supposedly curative powers. During the 19th century, a spa town, Hot Springs, was established here.

But in 1950, in a cheerfully brazen bid for fame that seems, somehow, very American, the town garnered nationwide publicity when it renamed itself Truth or Consequences after the popular radio show. The show's host, Ralph Edwards, has returned to T or C (as it is commonly known) faithfully, year

Antonio, lie 57,000 acres of grassland, upland desert and shimmering marshland devoted to the Bosque del Apache National Wildlife Refuge. From November through February, thousands of waterfowl winter here: snow geese with their pearly bodies and black-tipped wings; long-legged, long-beaked lesser sandhill cranes; a variety of ducks; and, rarest of all, a mere handful of that endangered species, the whooping crane. Here as part of an experiment designed to bring them back from near-extinction by putting their eggs in the nests of the sandhill cranes, the whoopers—although small in number—stand out in the throng of nearly 300 bird species that frequent the Bosque del Apache. At nearly five feet, they are the tallest American bird, snow white, with bare red faces and crowns; their distinctive whooping call is said to be audible for up to two miles.

The Bosque del Apache is particularly beautiful as day wanes, when the flocks return to the marshlands from their feeding grounds to the north. Then the wavering black lines of the homing birds are silhouetted against skies streaked with

DAN PEHA

after year, to participate in what is surely one of the oddest events in a nation devoted to the bizarre: the Ralph Edwards Fiesta, a raucous conglomeration of parades, contests, tournaments, barbecues and parties. In gratitude, T or C has named a park and erected a wax statue in the town museum to honor Edwards, its adopted local hero.

South of Truth or Consequences, the flood plain of the Rio Grande widens into the Mesilla Valley, its fertile, river-irrigated soils boasting the year-round crops of chile and cotton, orchards of pecan trees, and acres of vineyards that have been the traditional mainstay of southwestern New Mexico's largest city, Las Cruces (see page 98: Red Fire, Blue Corn). A lively, burgeoning business center and home to New Mexico State University, Las Cruces grew up around the thicket of wooden crosses for which it was named: grave markers for a party of travellers ambushed by the Apache in the days of the Camino Real.

The city is set at the foot of the astonishing Organ Mountains, so called because their craggy granite outcrops reminded the early Spanish explorers of organ pipes. Twenty-seven million years old, they rise abruptly from the smooth valley floor, a cresting wave of deeply eroded vertical joints and fissures. A certain aura of mystery surrounds these peaks: the Lost Padre Mine, a legendary lode of gold, is reputedly hidden somewhere in their deepest recesses (which have been mined extensively, with varying degrees of success); Sheriff Pat Garrett, the man who shot Billy the Kid, was himself shot to death here under still unexplained circumstances; and today, the mystery continues, with much of the Organs rendered an inaccessible part of the White Sands Missile Range.

Just across the Rio Grande from Las Cruces, still within sight of the high-crested Organs, lies La Mesilla, a small town with a peculiar history. In 1850, after the Mexican War had given the United States control of the New Mexico Territory, a group of Las Cruces townspeople who wished to remain citizens of Mexico moved across the river to start a settlement—La Mesilla—in their desired homeland. In 1853, they received a Mexican land grant, and their continuing Mexican citizenship seemed assured. But in 1854, with the signing of the Gadsden Purchase (not coincidentally, in La Mesilla itself), the little community was handed back to the United

MOGOLLON CULTURE

TOM TILL

Mogollon masonry dwellings sheltered by natural caves, Gila Cliff Dwellings National Monument.

Precursors to the highly developed Anasazi peoples of northern New Mexico, the people of the Mogollon Culture—named for the mountains in southwestern New Mexico where many of their remains have been discovered—emerged in New Mexico some 2,000 to 3,000 years ago. Initially nomads, they gradually adopted a more sedentary way of living, utilizing agricultural methods and crops (primarily corn, beans and squash) adopted from the more advanced cultures of ancient Mexico.

By 300 B.C., the Mogollon had become true farmers, and began to build permanent villages of earth-and-timber pit houses, their floors usually 10 to 40 inches below ground level; most villages also contained a larger pit house for ceremonial purposes. But perhaps the most important development of all was that, by this period, the Mogollon had learned to make pottery; they were the first people in the southwest to do so.

From the start, Mogollon pottery was well made: good utilitarian ware for cooking, carrying water and storing grain. It is significant, however, that the Mogollon also used their pottery for sacramental purposes, often burying pots as offerings with the dead. Such pots have been found among pit burial remains, each with a hole intentionally punched out of its base; anthropologists speculate that this was done to release the pot's spirit, thought to be part of its maker.

By the latter part of the first millenium A.D., the Mogollon had shared agricultural methods and pottery with their Anasazi neighbors to the north; the Anasazi had taken these gifts and gone on to surpass the Mogollon, becoming master farmers, engineers, craftspeople and city builders: the dominant culture in the Southwest. The Mogollon, in turn, had learned from the Anasazi, first building pit houses with masonry walls, then moving on to construct characteristically Anasazi-style multi-storied dwellings; some of the best-preserved examples of the latter building type may be seen at the Gila Cliff Dwellings National Monument.

But although Mogollon civilization declined as the Anasazi star rose, there was one cultural form where the Mogollon remained unsurpassed. During what archaeologists classify as the Mimbres Period of their development—from about 1050 to 1200 A.D.—they crafted a black-and-white ceramic ware that is considered the zenith of what is, perhaps, North America's most highly developed native art.

Unlike the beautiful but stylized work of the Anasazi, Mogollon pottery of the Mimbres Period was characterized by lively, often humorous decorations depicting human, animal and insect forms. A bat, balancing on tiny feet, will display its magnificently ornamented outstretched wings and seem to sneer with pride. Two young men, their faces ritualistically painted, their hair bound with intricately designed headbands, stare out, their expressions quizzical. All this, with an attention to detail and liveliness of line found only in the highest of high art.

The Mogollon people, like the Anasazi, mysteriously abandoned their homes sometime around the beginning of the 14th century, dying out, joining other tribes, drifting into the unknown. But their pottery is their testament; it offers, as the early Mogollon potters knew, a direct connection to the spirit of its makers.

States and its townspeople found themselves the victims of one of history's practical jokes.

Although the town grew and prospered until the 1880s, serving as a major stop on the Butterfield Overland Stage line, it declined after the Southern Pacific Railroad bypassed it in favor of neighboring Las Cruces. Today, as La Mesilla State Monument, it survives as an architectural treasure, its adobe-lined plaza displaying much the same general appearance as it did a century ago. The shops that fill those adobes, however, along with the crowds of tourists that throng them, present a far different picture; here again, it seems, the Anglo influence has prevailed over the Hispanic.

An historical oddity of another kind is commemorated to the southwest, at Columbus, just over the border from Mexico. There, just before dawn on March 9, 1916, Mexican revolutionary Pancho Villa led a band of guerrillas in an attack on the sleepy town of Columbus and its military outpost, Camp Furlong. Quickly repulsed, this quixotic attack nevertheless took the lives of 18 Americans and was the only time since the War of 1812 that the continental United States was invaded by foreign troops. Moreover, it precipitated the first use of air power for warfare: when General John J. "Black Jack" Pershing led a retaliatory party of 6,000 soldiers into Mexico, he was given air cover by eight single-engine planes from Fort Sam Houston in Texas. Pancho Villa State Park features many restored relics of the attack, plus a few remaining buildings from Camp Furlong. P.S.: Villa escaped.

West of Las Cruces, the Rio Grande Valley gives way to broad expanses of desert country punctuated by the scattered peaks of numerous small volcanic ranges. This was the route west of the Butterfield Overland Stage, but while much of the landscape is as magnificently vast and barren as it was more than a century ago, a great deal of it would be unrecognizable to the stagecoach travellers of old. The desert around Deming, for example, blooms today—thanks to the miracle of modern irrigation—with glistening fields of lettuce, cotton and grain.

On the other hand, there is the City of Rocks, a strange and timeless western Stonehenge once favored by Chiricahua Apache lying in wait to ambush the Butterfield stagecoaches. Now a state park, the City is a cluster of monumental formations sculpted by wind and rain from volcanic tuff.

(continued on page 100)

TOM CUSTER

KENT & DONNA DANNEN

Above: *The mysterious "organ pipe" outcrops of the Organ Mountains loom over equally mysterious ruins near Las Cruces.*
Left: *Units of the National Radio Astronomy Observatory's Very Large Array, placed on the Plains of San Agustin to gather signals from interstellar space.*

97

DENNIS & MARIA HENRY

RED FIRE, BLUE CORN

Until recently, travelers to New Mexico usually expected to dine out on standard "Mexican" fare, that generic, heavily Anglo-cized hodge-podge of tacos, refried beans and rice that can be hot to the tongue although not often flavorful to the palate. But with the recent growth of interest in native American cuisines, with menus across the nation studded with such dishes as Cajun popcorn, Shaker lemon pie and New England boiled dinner, food fanciers have become aware that New Mexico, too, offers its own indigenous cuisine, shaped by the region's centuries of isolation and multi-cultural influences into something piquant, varied and utterly distinctive.

New Mexican cuisine has its foundations in the simple crops raised first by Native Americans, then by the Spanish, all grown under irrigation and well suited to the region's generally mild, dry climate. First among these is *Capsicum frutescens,* the noble

Chile ristras hang to dry in the sun at Rancho de Chimayo.

chile, often referred to as "red fire," although most varieties are green when picked, turning yellow, orange, then red as they mature and dry. Columbus found chiles growing in the West Indies in 1493 and mistakenly called them peppers; they are, in fact, a member of the nightshade family, and thus related to such common items as tomatoes, potatoes and eggplant.

Some historians believe that conquering Spaniards introduced the chile to New Mexico from South or Central America, but there is conflicting evidence showing that the Pueblo Indians were already growing the pungent pods along the banks of the New Mexican Rio Grande when the Spaniards first arrived in the 16th century. Whatever its origins, whoever had it first, the chile has been used as the basis for New Mexican cookery for at least four centuries; the state today produces more chiles than all the other United States combined, and its per capita consumption of the vegetable is greater than any other region's. Among New Mexico's loveliest sights are the long red strings of chile ristras that appear everywhere each fall; hung to dry in the sun, they glow with warm color against brown adobe walls.

Richly flavored, in varieties ranging from mild to extra-hot, the chile's pungency derives from capsaicin, a bitter compound in the flesh and clear white seeds. Chiles are a rich source of Vitamins A and C, and they are reputedly an excellent preservative, retarding the oxidation of fats and delaying rancidity. They are most commonly used in the concoction of sauces: green, made from fresh chopped chiles, or red, compounded with ground dried chiles. The controversy over which sauce is hotter, red or green, is a red (or green) herring: either sauce can be hotter, depending on the variety of chile that goes into it.

Among the more characteristic chile dishes are (of course) chili, the ubiquitous western stew made in meat-studded or vegetarian versions, with or without beans (and try telling the creator of one particular style of chili that there is any other way to make it); chiles rellenos, fresh green chiles stuffed with cheese or a well seasoned meat mixture, then dipped in batter and lightly fried; and the piquant ruby- or emerald-colored chile jellies.

Another key ingredient of New Mexican cuisine is corn (*Zea mays*), native to the Americas and grown in New Mexico by the Pueblo Indians' prehistoric ancestors as early as 3000 to 2000 B.C. For the Pueblos, corn has been (and continues to be) more than a dietary staple; it plays an important part in tribal ceremonies, and is honored in such seasonal rites as the Corn Dance.

Corn is grown in an astonishing variety of hues: white, yellow, red, black, multi-colored and, of course, the popular blue. Ground into meal or flour (*masa harina*), it can be used to produce tortillas, the bread of New Mexico, which in turn are wrapped around a variety of fillings and prepared in different ways to make tacos, enchiladas and burritos; one of the tortilla's purest incarnations is the crispy tostado: the simple chip. Corn is also used in New Mexico in the preparation of tamales (corn meal stuffed with meat and red chile, wrapped in corn husks and then steamed in a chile preparation) and the awesomely flavorful *posole* (a stew made of hominy—lime-processed corn kernels—pork and red chiles).

Note must be made of the recent trendiness of blue corn. With tortillas and chips of dusky azure readily available in stores all over the country, the trend seems to be mounting almost to mania. This writer has even seen blue corn popcorn (it pops up white) and eaten blue corn pancakes (delicious); neither of these experiences, it should be admitted, took place in New Mexico. Blue corn is said to be more nutritious (with its additional niacin, protein, calcium and riboflavin) than white or yellow corn, and its flavor is distinctive, slightly nutty. But in this author's considered opinion, it is that odd, "oh-so-chic" color that is the source of blue corn's new popularity: pure aesthetics, nothing more—nor less.

Then there is the simple bush bean (*Phaseolus vulgaris*); in New Mexico, this usually means the pinto bean, a creamy little thing with the dark speckles that inspired its name. Plain, even common, the pinto bean in the hands of a New Mexican chef can nevertheless yield some inspiring dishes—and so good for you, too! Combined (as it usually is) with small amounts of meat or cheese, it constitutes what nutritionists call a perfect protein; it is, additionally, a source of iron, the B-complex vitamins and fiber.

Like chiles and corn, pinto beans have been a staple New Mexican crop for centuries; a canyon in Bandelier National Monument where the Pueblo Indians' Anasazi ancestors cultivated them is named in their honor: Frijoles Canyon. And like corn, the beans continue to play an important role in modern Pueblo life, both nutritionally and ceremonially.

New Mexican beans are rarely re-fried (a typical treatment elsewhere); most often they are presented as an elegantly spiced side dish, heady with the added flavors of chile and garlic. They are also used to stuff tortillas, fortify soups and stews, and even—combined with apples—as the basis for a highly unusual spice cake.

No discussion of New Mexican cuisine would be complete without mention of *sopaipillas*, mouth-watering concoctions that have been described as a kind of fry-bread, or perhaps a Hispanicized popover. Disregard the comparisons; sopaipillas are exactly what their name implies—little pillows—and they are unlike anything else. Light, puffed with air, these little squares of pastry, usually laden with honey, are a pure luxury, the unexpectedly perfect accompaniment to the heartiest New Mexican fare.

LEFT: GEORGE WUERTHNER; BELOW: TOM CUSTER

Above: Past a juniper-snagged ridge of the Florida Mountains, the panorama is a stark one of rocks, plains and sky.
Right: The remnants of a Mogollon mine scar the landscape near Silver City.

Facing page: The Middle Fork of the Gila River, a wildly beautiful corner of the Gila Wilderness.

Their rounded forms interspersed with the equally sculptural shapes of desert junipers, the rocks cast fantastic shadows; and in places on their surface, one can still see spots worn smooth by the grindstones of the patient Apache, getting a little work done as they waited for their quarry.

Southeast, at the base of the rugged Florida Mountains, is a rock fancier's heaven, Rock Hound State Park, where visitors are not only allowed but encouraged to take part of the park home with them. Collectors can make off with up to 15 pounds of the jasper, agate, quartz crystal and flow-banded rhyolite formed when groundwater deposited minerals in the park's rock cavities.

Far more precious was the yield of rocks to the north, where a series of mining towns boomed, flourished and—mostly—died during the last half of the 19th century.

Spaniards had discovered and mined copper in southwestern New Mexico as early as 1798 (at Santa Rita, where an enormous open-pit mine still produces copper ore), but it was not until the 1860s that the boom really got under way, with strike after strike of gold and silver at Piños Altos, Shakespeare, Silver City, Kingston, Hillsboro, Lake Valley and Mogollon.

Tent cities sprang up overnight to accommodate the steady influx of fortune-seekers working such evocatively named mines as the Solitaire, the Legal Tender, the U.S. Treasury, the Bridal Chamber, the Little Fanny, the Last Chance and the Confidence. Typically, these raw mining towns were wide-open and lawless; customers at tent-hotels would compete for lower bunks, considered safer than the uppers, where they might be caught by bullets flying from the proliferating local saloons.

Initially curtailed by constant Apache raids and the distractions of the Civil War, mining activities in the region nevertheless continued apace until the end of the century, producing millions of dollars worth of gold, silver, copper, lead, zinc and iron ores. But many of the lodes played out quickly, and those that didn't had to contend with other problems: the shortage of water that limited placer mining, the difficulty in tracing ore veins that hampered lode mining and—until the development of the railroads in the 1880s—the lack of a reliable transportation system.

In 1893, the bottom dropped out of the silver market—the mainstay of New Mexican mining—and most of the boom towns withered. With the exception of Silver City—today a thriving community with an economy broadly based on shipping, cattle ranching, education and, still, copper mining—they were abandoned to the winds. Some—Hillsboro and Kingston among them—have lately experienced revivals, their picturesque old buildings, now restored, filled with shops and residences of artists and others attracted by the former boom towns' historic charms. But most remain only as ghost towns, their fallen structures and gaping mine shafts dim reminders of southwestern New Mexico's brief heyday as a motherlode.

A ghost town of a different sort lies north of Silver City, in the rough and broken terrain of the region's volcanic highlands. Here, 180 feet up a steep talus slope, are a series of natural caves carved from porous layers of ash and lava by the eroding forces of wind and water. Around 700 years ago, people of the Mogollon Culture (see page 96) found their way to these sheltering alcoves, using them as a base for the construction of several adobe and timber structures containing some 42 rooms.

Today comprising the Gila Cliff Dwellings National Monument, these Mogollon ruins still display haunting evidence of their former life, their ceilings blackened by the smoke of ancient fires, their floors worn smooth in spots by the grinding stones of their old inhabitants. Once, the cliff dwellers made pots of exquisite craftsmanship, shaped finely worked obsidian spear points and arrowheads, and raised crops of corn, squash, beans and tobacco along the stream flowing at the base of their cliff. But early in the 14th century, they abandoned their mountain stronghold, for reasons yet—and perhaps forever—unknown.

The Gila Cliff Dwellings National Monument lies at the edge of the Gila Wilderness, America's first designated wilderness area. Established in 1924 (largely through the efforts of naturalist Aldo Leopold, whose *Sand County Almanac* and other writings are pioneering examples of environmental literature), this is a 200,000-acre expanse of nature in the raw, its rugged mountains and broad panoramas virtually untouched by the hand of man. Like so much of southwestern New Mexico, it is—as it always has been—adventurers' country, its wild beauty both a seduction and a challenge.

JONATHAN A. MEYERS

CENTRAL

DUKE CITY AND THE RING OF HISTORY

CHAPTER EIGHT

JUSTINE HILL

Above: Luminarias in Old Town Plaza, Albuquerque.

Facing page: Even big cities may have their charms: Albuquerque at dusk, viewed from Sandia Peak.

In 1936, archaeologists working in the Sandia Mountains discovered remnants of three separate human habitations, layered one on top of the other in a sheltered cave at the northeast end of this range, the backbone of New Mexico's central region. Pre-Columbian Pueblo-style artifacts were unearthed from the top, or most recent layer. Farther down, finely worked Folsom spear points—much like those discovered near Folsom in northeastern New Mexico—were found scattered among the bones of extinct bison, mammoths, giant sloths and ancestors of modern horses and camels. The deepest, oldest layer revealed more such bones, strewn this time with a cruder type of spear point: the work of perhaps the earliest New Mexican, now known as Sandia Man.

This kind of historical juxtaposition is not uncommon in New Mexico, and particularly here at the heart of the state, the hub of events from prehistoric times, through the Spanish conquest and the development of the western frontier, and on into our own era. For several centuries now, the area's focal point has been Albuquerque, but the state's dominant city is ringed with sites that bear witness to an even more distant past.

To the north, for example, where the cottonwood-shaded Rio Grande waters the fields of the peaceful farming community of Bernalillo, is Coronado State Monument, a conglomeration of archaeological finds attesting to several thousand years of human activity. Originally established to mark the site of the Pueblo village where Coronado may have made his expeditionary headquarters in the winter of 1540, the monument contains restored ruins of the village kiva, particularly notable for its polychrome murals of animal and human forms. Fortuitously, prior to construction of shelters in the adjacent Coronado State Park, archaeologists discov-

ered the foundations of a hacienda burned during the Pueblo Revolt of 1680. Further investigations ensued, revealing several even older finds: fire pits believed to have been used by nomadic Indians as early as 2000 to 3000 years B.C.

To the east, beyond the limestone-capped granite of the Manzano Mountains, lie other ruins, perhaps even more haunting. Here, Pueblo Indians of the 12th through 14th centuries constructed three substantial villages: Abo, Quarai and Gran Quivira. Utilizing local limestone at Gran Quivira and red sandstone at Abo and Quarai, these proficient masons got full value from natural joints in the rocks, which allows them to break easily into thin, nearly rectangular blocks. Spaniards found these pueblos on the salt flats of the Estancia Basin, and called the region *salinas*—salty; the ruins of the three villages today are administered as the Salinas National Monument.

Joining the monument's Pueblo remnants are the remains of several mission churches built by the Franciscans during the 17th century. La Purisima Concepcion, at Quarai, was reputed to be especially magnificent, with walls some 40 feet high and four to five feet thick. Strong as it was, this church—and indeed, all of the three villages—were fatally situated on the eastern flank of the Manzanos; there, exposed to the plains, they were overrun by fierce nomadic Indians. Quarai, it seems, was subject to a particularly brutal and sudden attack: the remains of bodies cut down in the midst of everyday activities have been found there, indicating that the village was taken utterly by surprise. Survivors (faced also by a severe drought in the 1670s) abandoned Abo, Quarai and Gran Quivira; they are known today as "The Cities that Died of Fear."

A happier trio of ghost towns stud the Turquoise Trail,

RICHARD B. LEVINE

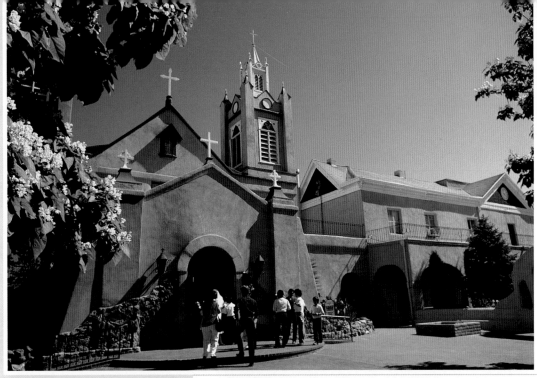

ABOVE: KENT & DONNA DANNEN; BELOW: VIRGINIA FERRERO

Above: A First Communion procession on its way into San Felipe de Neri Church, the centerpiece of Albuquerque's Old Town.
Right: Albuquerque's 640-acre University of New Mexico campus boasts buildings designed in a modified Pueblo style.

Facing page: Sandia Peak Aerial Tram, the world's longest continuous tramway, offers magnificent views as it climbs to the Sandia summit.

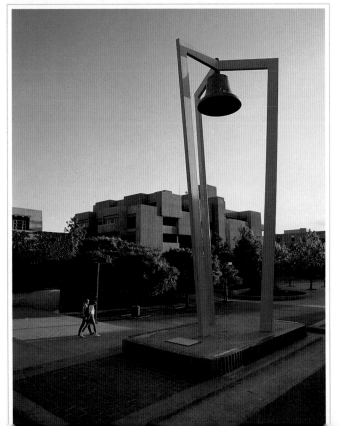

running through the Cerillos Hills between Albuquerque and Santa Fe, where the shacks and shanties of former mining communities Cerillos, Madrid and Golden have been cheerfully refurbished to house shops and residences. A mining district from prehistoric times, the Turquoise Trail area was, as its name indicates, particularly rich in turquoise, a gemstone, that forms as nuggets or thin crusts deposited by subterranean water circulating through certain kinds of volcanic rock. The turquoise found here is of particularly high quality, its distinctive sky-blue color deriving from minute quantities of copper compounds.

First mined by local Indians (who attributed spiritual significance to the stone), then by Spaniards, turquoise gave way toward the end of the 19th century to gold, silver, lead and coal; with the mineral strikes came the boom towns. Cerillos was the leading town of the district, boasting eight newspapers, several hotels and 21 saloons, one of which sold a shot of whiskey for the tariff of three pinches of gold dust. Golden, which had the customary sampling of saloons, a post office and even a stock exchange, was cursed by a perennial housing shortage; its miners were forced to camp out in the surrounding hills or even take up residence in such odd dwellings as an unused coke oven. Madrid lasted longest, serving as a coal company town until the 1950s. Then it, like its fellows, was abandoned to the elements, its long rows of identical company-built houses left to fall into ruins.

In the 1970s, however, the gentrifiers, restoration enthusiasts and craftspeople moved in; today the three quasi-ghost towns sport a growing selection of shops and homes, often inhabited by commuters who drive the short distances to Santa Fe or Albuquerque. These last enjoy the best of both worlds: a tranquil small-town existence, and the undeniable excitement and diversity offered by life in the big city.

In New Mexico, "big city" can mean only one thing: Albuquerque. With a population hovering near the half-million mark, it is the state's leading center for business, medicine, scientific research and development and other high-tech industries. But this friendly giant began as a tiny farming community, founded by just 35 families who decided to take a flyer in response to a governmental decree.

In 1706, soon after Don Diego De Vargas's reconquest of New Mexico, messengers from Mexico City fanned out into provincial settlements scattered up and down the valley of the Rio Grande, soliciting colonizers for a new villa being established at the base of the Sandia Mountains. The town was to be called San Francisco de Alburquerque, after the Duke of Alburquerque, Viceroy of New Spain; the Duke, a prudent man, renamed it to include his sovereign, King Philip of Spain. Thus, the new town started life as San Felipe de Alburquerque; but the King would not be memorialized for long. In time, the town's name would be shortened, an "r" dropped; we know it today as Albuquerque, the Duke City.

Lured by bonuses of tools and livestock, Albuquerque's founding families were attracted also by the town's location in a broad basin on the eastern bank of the Rio Grande. There, river terraces over sedimentary rock yielded rich volcanic soil; crops and stock flourished. Valuable, too, was the protection from Indian attacks offered by the fortress-like cliffs of the overshadowing Sandia Range; 1.4-billion-year-old granite capped with more recent sedimentary limestone, these mountains cradle Albuquerque's eastern flank. Far to the west, marking the edge of the high plateau country, lie five lava-lapped cones, the Albuquerque volcanoes, inactive for millions of years. And to the north, the Rocky Mountains come to their two-pronged end in the nearly parallel ranges of the Jemez and Sangre de Cristo Mountains.

This stunning panorama may be seen today from Sandia Crest (at 10,678 feet the highest scenic drive in the Southwest) or (for those with a tolerance of heights) from the Sandia Peak Aerial Tram, the world's longest continuous tramway. The latter climbs 2.7 miles to the 10,360-foot Sandia Peak summit, whisking travelers through four of our continent's seven life zones: the biological equivalent of going from Mexico to Alaska in 20 minutes.

From the beginning, Albuquerque was a shipping and trading center, benefitting from its prominent location on the Camino Real between Mexico City and Santa Fe. By 1790, just 84 years after its founding, its population had soared to 6,000; in fact, except for the 1880s when Socorro sailed on its sea of silver, Albuquerque has always been New Mexico's largest city. During the 19th century, it continued to grow by leaps and bounds, first with the increased flow of Missouri traders' commercial goods over the Chihuahua Trail (a southern extension of the Santa Fe Trail, following essentially

THE RAILROAD

MUSEUM OF NEW MEXICO

A railroad crew lays the final stretch of track on the Santa Fe Central Rail Road, August 1903.

The first railroad company in America, the Baltimore and Ohio, was chartered in 1827. It was not until more than half a century later, however, that the first engine came steaming into New Mexico over Raton Pass, ending forever the region's centuries of isolation and irretrievably altering its economy, appearance and character.

Two companies had engaged in a fierce competition to be the first to lay track in this virgin terrain: the Atchison, Topeka & Santa Fe, originally a Kansas short line (the Atchison & Topeka) whose directors optimistically added the "Santa Fe" as they moved into Colorado and eagerly looked south; and the Denver & Rio Grande, incorporated with the intention of moving on to Santa Fe, El Paso and eventually Mexico. Both companies had their eyes on the Raton Pass; reaching heights of nearly 8,000 feet, this rocky gap in the Southern Rockies presented a formidable challenge, one that would require both careful surveying and expensive construction work.

The company that was first to file a survey and then occupy the pass with work crews would win the coveted route; the two railroads jockeyed for position. The Denver had an advantage in that it was a narrow-gauge line, and so could lay track over mountainous terrain far more cheaply than could the broad-gauge Santa Fe. But the Santa Fe had civil engineer William Raymond Morley. The former manager of the enormous Maxwell Land Grant, Morley knew northeastern New Mexico like the proverbial back of his hand; he also knew Uncle Dick Wootton, owner of the celebrated toll road through Raton Pass. Conspiring with Wootton, Morley disguised himself as a sheepherder and managed to survey Raton Pass without arousing the suspicions of various Denver-company spies posted in the area.

Armed with Morley's survey, the general manager of the Santa Fe rushed to the capital for which his company was named and in February of 1878 won from the legislature a territorial charter to bring the railroad into New Mexico. Aware now that their only hope for controlling Raton Pass was to lay track there ahead of the Santa Fe, the Denver company immediately dispatched a work crew to that critical spot on the New Mexico-Colorado border. But although the Denver crew traveled through the night, they arrived too late: Morley had once again enlisted the help of Uncle Dick. Together, the two men had commandeered the clientele of a saloon near the top of Raton Pass; provided with shovels, this rag-tag bunch formed the work crew that claimed the Pass—and New Mexico—for the Atchison, Topeka & Santa Fe. The railroad, incidentally, bought Uncle Dick's toll road, transforming the old mountain man into a gentleman of leisure.

Having won the territory, the Santa Fe company, soon joined by other railroads, proceeded to lay track at an astonishing rate, sometimes up to a mile and a half in a single day; almost one third of New Mexico's railroad track was laid in a period of just over two years. In 1881, the lines of the Santa Fe and the Southern Pacific Railroad met at Deming, in the southwestern portion of the state; this meant that a transcontinental route was now in place, connecting New Mexico to both east and west coasts. Typically, although they had achieved something significant for New Mexico, the two railroads remained bitter rivals for many years, maintaining separate wings at the Deming depot and running their schedules according to different time zones.

With the coming of the railroad, the face of New Mexico changed dramatically. New towns—Tucumcari, Lordsburg, Clayton and Clovis among them—sprang up overnight; established settlements, too, were transformed, either declining when the railroad bypassed them (like, say, Mesilla) or booming as a result of new, rail-carried commerce (as was the case with Roswell). A few towns literally doubled; Albuquerque had its New Albuquerque, Las Vegas its East Las Vegas, both fast-growing railroad-inspired communities that eventually swallowed up their adjoining Old Towns.

The railroad also broadened New Mexico's economic base, giving older industries, such as mining and ranching, the reliable transportation system they needed to realize their potentials, while introducing new trades and services. Chief among the latter was tourism. With writers such as Charles Lummis (the man who coined the phrase, "See America First") heralding the splendors of Hispanic Santa Fe and Taos, with the railroad-associated Fred Harvey Houses displaying Indian arts and crafts, and with railroad travel growing more comfortable and familiar by the day, pleasure-seekers began to flood into every previously remote, now enticingly exotic corner of the state. Many of them, caught by the region's charms, stayed on. And they, with the mountain men, cattle ranchers, miners and homesteaders who came before them, joined the descendants of Spanish conquistadors and Native Americans to shape modern New Mexico.

Right: Old Town Albuquerque, bypassed by the railroad, was swallowed up by "New" Albuquerque, fell almost to ruins, then was saved by determined preservationists.
Below: Atchison, Topeka & Santa Fe engine number 137, nicknamed "Baby," one of the first railroad engines into New Mexico, October 1880.

MUSEUM OF NEW MEXICO

DENNIS & MARIA HENRY

JONATHAN A. MEYERS

Above: Autumn along La Luz Trail in the Sandia Mountains' Cibola National Forest.

Facing page, top: Sunrise over Madrid, a former mining town on the Turquoise Trail now being revivified by gentrifiers, restorationists and Albuquerque commuters.
Bottom left: The National Atomic Museum at Kirtland Air Force Base, Albuquerque.
Bottom right: A buoyant ascension at the annual Albuquerque International Balloon Fiesta.

Old Town could not be destroyed, however; although it languished until well into this century, by the 1930s its plaza and surrounding homes had become the focus of a determined group of preservationists. They waged an energetic and ultimately successful campaign to save Old Town; today, restored, it constitutes Albuquerque's principal tourist attraction. Along its charming warren of narrow streets, tight clusters of softly rounded adobe buildings (see page 110: Adobe) now house a multitude of smart shops, galleries and restaurants. And the plaza's venerable church of San Felipe de Neri, where services have been held every day for nearly 300 years, is the historic and sentimental heart not just of Old Town, but of all of metropolitan Albuquerque, as well.

As a railroad boom town, the new Albuquerque initially played host to a motley crew of gamblers, gunfighters, confidence men and fortune-seekers who sported at a typical frontier conglomeration of barrooms and gambling halls, fandango palaces and tonsorial parlors, many of them open 24 hours a day. But this rowdy bunch soon gave way to a new breed: the settlers and homesteaders, businessmen and wage workers who often follow close on the heels of their wilder brethren, taming a town rather than breaking it.

Among the more salutary effects of such civilizing influences was the 1889 establishment in Albuquerque of one of New Mexico's first public colleges, the University of New Mexico. Today a highly respected center of education particularly notable for its programs in anthropology and Southwestern studies, the University occupies a 640-acre campus, its buildings handsomely designed in a modified Pueblo style. The campus is home to the New Mexico Symphony Orchestra, the world-renowned Tamarind Institute of Lithography and the Maxwell Museum of Anthropology, an outstanding collection of exhibits about early man with an emphasis on native cultures of the Southwest.

In the 1890s, the Societe Medicale of Paris conducted a survey of world climates, concluding that New Mexico's provided "more beneficial characteristics and fewer drawbacks than any other region of the world." Accordingly, health-seekers began to pour into the region, and Albuquerque took its place as a major medical center, its clear, dry air promising relief to people suffering from tuberculosis, asthma and other respiratory ailments. The first tuberculosis sanitar-

the same route as the Camino Real); then, after 1846, when a military post was established there by General Stephen Kearny, who had claimed the New Mexico Territory for the United States. Its status as an Army town made Albuquerque a glittering prize during the Civil War; it was occupied by the Confederates for two months in 1862, until they were forced to retreat, soundly beaten, after the Battle of Glorieta Pass.

The coming of the railroad in 1880 marked a turning point for Albuquerque, as it did for so much of previously isolated New Mexico (see page 106). Almost as soon as the first spikes were driven east of the Plaza, the town's already burgeoning population doubled; in fact, the town itself doubled, in a repetition of events that lately had occurred to the northeast, at Las Vegas. A new Albuquerque sprang up around the railroad depot, some two miles from what then became known as Old Town; soon, the two towns were connected by a horse-drawn streetcar, and eventually the upstart community engulfed the original settlement.

ium, founded in 1902 by the Sisters of Charity, was followed by numerous others, most of them located along a stretch of the town's main thoroughfare soon dubbed "T.B. Avenue." Many patients fell in love with New Mexico and, recovered, stayed on to further swell the ranks of Albuquerque's population.

Since the 1930s, more than a hundred federal agencies have been established in Albuquerque; this, along with the development of Kirtland Air Force Base and the Sandia National Laboratories (a private corporation which began as a subsidiary of the Los Alamos National Laboratory) during World War II, added fuel to the fire of the city's growth. Kirtland today is an Air Force Special Weapons Center, engaged in weapons research; Sandia is a defense contractor specializing in the research and development of nuclear weapons, although it is also at work trying to discover new and improved sources of energy. The importance of the defense industry to Albuquerque's economic, social and intellectual makeup cannot be underestimated.

Today, one third of New Mexico's population lives in Albuquerque, and the town has its concomitant share of big-city woes: crime, too much development and too little planning, excruciating pockets of poverty existing side by side with glittering monuments to conspicuous consumption. Often, the city's greatest strength—its tripartite Indian-Hispanic-Anglo culture—is the source of its greatest tensions.

But somehow, the Duke City's strong ties to its past and the forceful, unforgettable presence of its beautiful natural environment go a long way towards offsetting these ills. Albuquerque may sprawl, but it does so amiably; its character is relaxed, its attitude positive: problems can be resolved, solutions are available. It seems fitting that the city's newly adopted symbol is the hot-air balloon, hundreds of which gather each October for the mass ascensions of the Albuquerque International Balloon Fiesta, the world's largest hot-air ballooning event. It is a breathtaking sight: dozens of brilliantly colored, softly shaped balloons wafting upward against the city's glowing turquoise skies. They paint a picture that is buoyant, optimistic, ever on-the-rise, like Albuquerque itself, and like the state for which the city serves as both emblem and avatar: that veritable land of enchantment, New Mexico.

DENNIS & MARIA HENRY

KENT & DONNA DANNEN

KENT & DONNA DANNEN

ADOBE

If there is one thing that sets New Mexico apart from other regions, instantly marking it as "different," it is its architecture, distinguished by the softly colored, gently undulating forms characteristic of only one building material: adobe.

Although the word "adobe" is Spanish and Arabic, the Indians of New Mexico were utilizing the local sandy clay in construction for many centuries before the conquest. Starting with a thick mixture of mud strengthened by the addition of stones, grasses or even pottery shards, they built walls by the manipulation of the clay into courses, or layers, allowing each course to dry before applying the next, a handful of mud at a time.

Along with a new name, Spanish colonists introduced several innovations in the making of adobe. Chief among these was the use of wooden forms to mold adobe bricks which were then dried and hardened in the sun; stacked and mortared with more adobe, such bricks were both easier to build with and more durable. Their durability was further enhanced by the addition to the clay mixture of straw, a strengthening agent which also served to wick moisture—adobe's deadliest enemy—away from the cen-

ter of each brick. Properly maintained, an adobe structure can last for centuries, a fact to which New Mexico's many 17th-century adobes (houses, mission churches, even Santa Fe's venerable Palace of the Governors) clearly attest.

The classic Spanish adobe house was built by both men and women, with men doing the heavy labor while women provided the final, more "artistic" touches. Laid on a stone foundation, the adobe walls would rise to a ceiling intricately constructed of diagonally laid planks or sapling twigs (*latillas*) and supported by massive beams (*vigas*), usually of peeled pine or fir. Roofs looked flat, but were slightly tilted to provide drainage (also aided by the use of wooden *canales,* or drainage spouts), and were constructed of layers of brush, adobe and eight or more inches of dirt.

Once the men had built the basic structure, women moved in to plaster the exterior walls with more adobe, which might vary in color (depending on the source of clay) from white to red to a warm brown. Interior walls were also plastered, then washed with thin layers of natural earthen paint (another form of adobe) in such hues as *tierra bayeta* (a soft fawn) or *tierra blanca* (white decoratively flecked with mica). Women were additionally responsible for the construction of gently rounded corner fireplaces and for the laying of floors, sometimes simply earthen, sometimes spread with more adobe, sometimes soaked with animal blood for hardness.

Often starting life as one-room houses, adobes were typically added to, room by room, as families grew and prospered. Larger homes were often built around an inner courtyard, with rooms opening to the outside and connected with walkways shaded by portals, or porches, supported by wooden columns and corbels. Because earlier residences also had to serve as fortresses against frequent Indian raids, and because glass was generally unavailable, they had few windows; those that existed were small and frequently barred.

As the settlements grew more secure, villagers had time to decorate and embellish their homes; this they did with an individuality—and often, a whimsicality—that has evolved into a design tradition. Adobe was now used sculpturally, to shape rounded surfaces and stepped walls; *nichos* (niches) were introduced in both interior and exterior walls to hold carvings, candlesticks and other items of the household treasury. A house's wooden elements—doors, window frames, gates, bars, columns and corbels—were often intricately carved with scrolls, rosettes, shells and geometric designs. The adobe emerged as one large, elaborate, very personal work of art.

With the coming of the railroad to territorial New Mexico, however, the style fell into disfavor, largely—it must be said—because of the initial Anglo distaste for native forms of expression. Ranks of adobe houses were jumbled side by side with—or replaced by—brick or frame variations on Midwestern Victoriana. Those adobes that remained were often altered by the addition of brick coping (a key element of the so-called Territorial Style), metal roofs, gables, dormers and gingerbread trim.

But things took a turn for the better with the arrival of another Anglo influence: that of the artists who began to flock to the art colonies of Taos and Santa Fe around the turn of the century. Powerfully drawn to the traditional building styles they found in New Mexico, many bought and renovated old adobe homes, contributing decorative painting and carving of their own invention, as well as reviving indigenous styles. Adobe architecture thus shared in the general renaissance of native arts and crafts that has burgeoned in New Mexico since the 1920s.

With the proliferation of the so-called "Santa Fe Style," adobe has never been more popular than it is today, not only in New Mexico, but nation-wide. In these days of diminishing resources, it provides a building material of infinite supply; its ability to retain temperature also gives it excellent passive solar capacities. Commercial adobe yards now produce a stabilized adobe brick, its mud mixed with an additive that enhances its ability to resist moisture. Although adobe is no longer a cheap material (due to the amount of labor involved in making and setting the bricks), its many other qualities offset its initial expense.

Ultimately, there is its beauty. Its smooth, luminous surfaces and strong, sculptural shapes are unexcelled in any other architecture. Adobe provides the most essentially human form of dwellingplace, crafted by hand to shelter its maker.

ABOVE AND FACING PAGE: MUSEUM OF NEW MEXICO

Above: An adobe brick "farm," circa 1945.
Below: Architecture as sculpture: the sinuous adobe lines of the Museum of Fine Arts, Santa Fe.

Facing page: Pueblo women hand-plastering an adobe wall, Sandoval County, October 1936.

DENNIS & MARIA HENRY

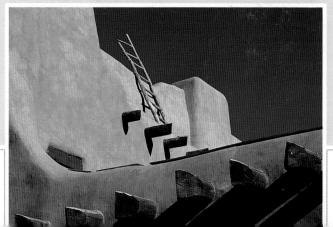

FOR FURTHER READING

Armstrong, Ruth. *Enchanted Trails*. Santa Fe: New Mexico Magazine, 1980. An official town-by-town, attraction-by-attraction guidebook.

Calvin, Ross. *Sky Determines*. Albuquerque: University of New Mexico Press, 1948. A Southwest classic, historical, ecological and philosophical.

Casey, Robert L. *Journey to the High Southwest*. Seattle: Pacific Search Press, 1986. Fascinating guide to the Four Corners region.

Chronic, Halka. *Roadside Geology of New Mexico*. Missoula, Mont.: Mountain Press Publishing Company, 1987. The indispensable guide to New Mexico geology. Lavishly detailed, clearly written: a must.

Church, Peggy Pond. *The House at Otowi Bridge*. Albuquerque: University of New Mexico Press, 1959. The poetically-told story of Edith Warner, a woman who bridged the disparate worlds of San Ildefonso Indians and Los Alamos scientists.

Douglas, Jim. *The Complete New Mexico Cookbook*. Albuquerque: Modern Press, 1977. Good collection of New Mexican recipes and lore.

Ellis, Richard N., editor. *New Mexico Past and Present*. Albuquerque: University of New Mexico Press, 1971. A historical reader, filled with fascinating essays on a variety of topics.

Franzwa, Gregory M. *Images of the Santa Fe Trail*. St. Louis: The Patrice Press, 1988. A modern photo study of landmarks on the historic trail.

Hillerman, Tony, editor. *The Spell of New Mexico*. Albuquerque: University of New Mexico Press, 1976. Gorgeous essays by such writers as Oliver La Farge, D.H. Lawrence, Conrad Richter and Tony Hillerman.

Houlihan, Patrick T., et al. *Harmony by Hand*. San Francisco: Chronicle Books, 1987. Fascinating essays on Southwestern Indian arts.

Jamison, Bill. *The Insider's Guide to Santa Fe*. Boston: The Harvard Common Press, 1987. Well written, comprehensive guide to the City Different.

Lavender, David. *The Southwest*. New York: Harper & Row, 1980. Colorful history, superbly anecdotal, with an emphasis on New Mexico and Arizona.

Long, Haniel. *Piñon Country*. Lincoln: University of Nebraska Press, 1986 (reprint). Historical and ecological essays, charmingly written.

Luhan, Mabel Dodge. *Edge of Taos Desert*. New York: Harcourt, Brace, 1937. An autobiographical account of Luhan's love affair with New Mexico.

Maxwell Museum of Anthropology. *Seven Families in Pueblo Pottery*. Albuquerque: University of New Mexico Press, 1975. Catalogue for a 1974 exhibition, tracing the development of pottery styles and offering fascinating interviews with potters.

Mays, Buddy. *Indian Villages of the Southwest*. San Francisco: Chronicle Books, 1985. An up-to-date, practical guide to the pueblos.

Morrill, Claire. *A Taos Mosaic*. Albuquerque: University of New Mexico Press, 1973. Personal essays about life in modern Taos.

Nichols, John. *If Mountains Die*. New York: Alfred A. Knopf, 1979. Beautifully written memoir by the well-known Taos-based novelist, with sumptuous photographs by William Davis.

Pike, Donald G. *Anasazi: Ancient People of the Rock*. Palo Alto: American West Publishing Company, 1974. Documentation of Anasazi ruins, with stunning photographs by David Muench.

Roberts, Calvin A. and Susan A. *New Mexico*. Albuquerque: University of New Mexico Press, 1988. Good basic history, very up to date.

Russell, Marian. *Land of Enchantment*. Albuquerque: University of New Mexico Press, 1981. Mrs. Russell's memoirs of life along the Santa Fe Trail, originally published in 1954.

Simmons, Marc, editor. *On the Santa Fe Trail*. Lawrence: University Press of Kansas, 1986. Memoirs and accounts of experiences on the trail.

Simmons, Marc. *New Mexico: An Interpretive History*. Albuquerque: University of New Mexico Press, 1988. Excellent history by one of New Mexico's leading men of letters.

Smith, Toby. *New Mexico Odyssey*. Albuquerque: University of New Mexico Press, 1987. Sketches by an award-winning Albuquerque journalist.

Wilson, Jane, and Charlotte Serber, editors. *Standing By and Making Do: Women of Wartime Los Alamos*. Los Alamos: The Los Alamos Historical Society, 1988. Memoirs of women who lived and worked in the secret Atomic City.